PERSONAL STORIES THAT INSPIRE AND MOTIVATE

ASPIRE TO INSPIRE

Forgive the Past • Live the Present • Create the Future

ABOUT THE PUBLISHER

Get Up and Go

Get Up and Go Publications Ltd, based in Sligo, Ireland, has produced The Irish Get Up and Go Diary every year since 2007. Eileen Forrestal and Brendan Sands have created a range of colourful, light and engaging diaries and journals to inspire and motivate all ages of readers to 'get up and go' in life. They also produce diaries for young people; a diary for busy women; and the Homework Journal for School Students. Their annual Get Up and Go event brings together inspirational speakers from all walks of life. Speakers at Get Up and Go events are courageous individuals who have stepped outside their own 'comfort zone', to share their experience of living life 'with passion and purpose'.

ISBN 978-1-910921-15-9

Published in Ireland by
GET UP AND GO PUBLICATIONS LTD
Email: info@getupandgodiary.com
www.getupandgodiary.com

Compiled by Eileen Forrestal
Edited by Cláir Ní Aonghusa
Graphic design by Nuala Redmond
Printed in Ireland by GPS Colour Graphics.

THE STORIES

FOREWORD
by
Judymay Murphy

There Be Heroes

Born onto the same planet, gifted with rewards and challenges, and the same 24 hours in each day, we share more than our diverse circumstances might at first suggest. And yet, no matter what the background, and in spite of fickle fate, some flourish, some flounder, while others abide in that zone of almost living, dutifully serving their structures instead of building out into the world the magnificence that lies expectantly within them.

So what does it take to rise up through your daily confusion, exhaustion and hopes and break through to being and experiencing all that is possible in this one life?

The most notable indicator of success (however broadly or specifically you wish to define this ideal) is the influence of those around you who themselves have reached high and burned brightly. Their standards and expectations for how a life might be well-lived are absorbed by you, often unknowingly. If you sit in the same room as them, they guide you quietly in the way their eyebrow raises when you share with them your latest action or inaction. If you reach out to them by insisting on living in ways that would have them nod and acknowledge you as part of the same active dream, a dream to evolve humanity, then seeing their earlier selves in you either excites or saddens them, depending on whether you've decided to join them on the upside or to simply let all that latent power wither away in the root, killed by caffeine, apathy, late night TV, and a story about being broken. A hero is someone who will subtly mirror back to you your own progress through a glow of light in their eye when you show up in courageous mode or, with a sigh, when they see you shrinking yourself to fit in with the dull and oft-damning herd.

Here in this book that started as the dream of one such mighty have-a-go hero, you will find gathered members of our eager tribe who have dared to expand themselves in human and beautiful ways. They all wish for you the lessons they have harvested, the cuts they have healed, and the victories they have celebrated. Their generosity of spirit and belief in all of us as a shaky yet valiant species sings through their stories. Gently and fiercely they've adventured within their own selves out in our shared world. By telling their stories thus far, they allow us all to remember why we're alive here today. Heroes abound, and here some have gathered to salute your road ahead.

One question I'm often asked as I trot the globe teaching the learnable art of success, is about how someone can know if they've reached their limits, or whether more lies dormant within, ready to be expressed? The answer already stands in the hungering nature of the question. Your knowing springs from those feelings of recognition and longing when you hear of someone having reached out for their own shot at glory, understanding that their story is yours, the only difference being that the paint is fully dry on theirs, the details fixed and recorded for all time, while yours is a work in progress or, at the very least, an awesome something yearning for release.

Many take the seemingly easier path of settling for what they currently are instead of stretching for who they might be. But if there's one thing I've learned through my past decade and a half as a coach and speaker around the world, it's that the hardest thing of all is to leave it too late to decide to be all you might be. To wake up surrounded by a mere fraction of the spiritual, material, intellectual and emotional treasures that have always waited patiently for you to embrace them, such is the only true tragedy we have to face in the end. A life unlived, a love unloved, a mind hopelessly folded in on itself, a height unscaled, a dream discarded - these are as tragic as they are unnecessary. It reminds me of this passage from the Gospel of Thomas, "If you bring forth what is within you, what you bring forth will save you. If you do not bring forth what is within you, what you do not bring forth will destroy you."

And one day there will be an end, there will be a time when it's too late to be all you might have been, but happily that day is not today. Today you will fill your well from the stories of others and drink from that well on your journey and, in turn, you will inspire the rest of us to even greater things. This is how it works. As you sow, water and reap you're creating a harvest that both feeds you and also provides seeds for those in need. This is how we best love.

Success is less about what you accumulate and more about what you gain in the process of building your kingdom. It's about who you become, what you will create, and how you will gift this planet in your own unique, perfectly imperfect ways.

Quite simply, this is a book about you, the you that will happen very soon.

Judymay Murphy is an Irish-born International Motivational Speaker and Success Coach, and the author of seven titles published in 28 countries. Over the past decade-and-a-half she has risen to the top ranks of speakers internationally and is known for her encouragement and training of many other speakers, teachers and healers.

"A hero is an ordinary individual who finds the strength to persevere and endure in spite of overwhelming obstacles."

CHRISTOPHER REEVE

ABOUT THE AUTHOR

Gordon Ryan

Growing up in Roscommon, Gordon Ryan coped reasonably well with his cystic fibrosis until it became life-threatening during his 20s. Despite successfully completing a law degree, Gordon's plans of establishing his career were foiled by frequent hospitalisations, repeated lung infections, oxygen use, deteriorating quality of life, and a total loss of independence. The call for a double lung transplant finally came through after three and a half years on a waiting list. His life transformed. Gordon is pursuing a full time Masters in Journalism (DCU). He is a passionate advocate for organ donation that saves and restores lives, and will soon launch an organ donation blog.

*"Just when the caterpillar thought life
was over it became a butterfly."*
ANONYMOUS

My Donor, My Hero

GORDON RYAN

Four years ago I was confined to a hospital room in the cystic fibrosis unit in St Vincent's University Hospital, dependent on a BiPap ventilator, that resembled a scuba diving mask strapped around my head, to push air into my lungs 24 hours a day, seven days a week, just to breathe.

Life was merely existence and struggle. Everyday matters like going to the shops, or enjoying a meal out, were no longer possible. Even climbing the stairs was too much as I was so breathless.

Looking out the window of that hospital room I often wondered what I did to deserve this. A prisoner in my body, I was trapped in end-stage respiratory failure. Having battled long and hard with the condition since my early 20s, life was on hold waiting for a life-saving transplant. There were two ways out of this nightmare, either with new lungs, or meeting my maker.

CF is Ireland's most common life threatening illness. There is no cure. People with it lack a protein in their gene type regulating the balance of salt and water in the cells of the lungs. Excess salt results, causing a sticky mucus. Repeated, severe lung infections scar lung tissue and progressively damage lung function. When one's lung function drops below 30%, a transplant is deemed the only hope of survival. In Ireland, life expectancy for somebody with CF is 31 years.

Growing up, I had little comprehension of the grim reality of my illness. Unlike some children with CF, I was not wrapped in cotton wool or restricted from doing stuff. My parents brought my sister and me up as normally as possible. CF was kept at arm's length.

I never felt any different to anybody else at school. My Mum often told me to make sure not to get cold or wet. My answer was, "There is nothing wrong with me." In my own head, I did not feel different from my peers. Looking back now, I see how I struggled to keep up playing football.

My normal upbringing worked for as long as I was holding my own and did not get sick. Everybody's pattern of illness varies, and I was fortunate to stay out of hospital for much of my early life.

Then CF reared its ugly head. At 21 years of age, I found myself stretched out in St Vincent's for six weeks with a nasty lung infection. That hospital admission was a defining moment, forcing me to confront this illness.

At the time I was in University in Galway studying Law, with plans and ambitions to fulfill. However, CF respects neither one's hopes nor one's dreams. This I learnt the hard way. It took a few years to accept having the condition.

I felt bitter and resentful that life was being constantly interrupted by an illness that refused to go away. I was sick and tired of the daily routine of self care, physiotherapy and nebulizers, and wished it gone.

The turning point came when an experienced nurse said, "Gordon, you need to remember one thing. CF is about looking after yourself and keeping well, as opposed to getting better." Thinking about it this way helped me to cope better. Realising that CF was part of me, and allowing for this, was crucial. I had CF, but CF did not have me.

After many years of recurrent lung infections resulting in hospitalisation, the issue of transplant was raised in 2009. My lung function was 26% and dropping. My reaction was terror. The prospect scared the hell out of me.

A double lung transplant is deemed necessary when the medics feel a person with CF will live longer with it than if they struggle on. As I saw it, nobody in their right mind would choose to undergo a transplant. However, at the back of my mind, I knew I did not have a choice as the odds are stacked against a person with end-stage CF. I could opt not to go on the list but, inevitably, that meant seeing out my time.

What I wanted more than anything was to live a life uninterrupted by constant illness and hospitalisation. A transplant offered me that hope. I was placed on the Newcastle transplant list in June 2010.

People would ask, "When are you getting your transplant?" Nobody actually had any idea. It's a lottery. You might get called that day, or never get a call. Getting on the list earlier meant giving yourself a better chance as the clock was ticking mercilessly. You did not know how much time you had left.

Friends ran out of time before and after getting on the list. Some delayed making a decision, and then got much worse. Seeing them pass away brought home to me how serious the situation was. At least I was giving myself a chance. But being on the list only meant my name being there. A match had to be right in terms of antibodies, blood type and size.

The personal battle was as much psychological as physical. The only element I could control was my attitude. Staying strong mentally was vital. Rather than lamenting all I could no longer do, my focus was on trying to do the few things I could still do. Otherwise I would have ended up in a very dark place.

A close friend, Marie, was not so fortunate. She and I often discussed transplant during mutual spells in hospital. She was sceptical. "It's somebody else's lungs isn't it?" I'd say, "Yes Marie, but if your own are no longer working, and you could receive a pair which do, why not go for it?"

Later Marie became pregnant. She stayed in hospital all that summer. Although very unwell, she gave birth to a beautiful baby boy. The pregnancy drained her so much that most of her time afterwards was spent in hospital.

One night she rang. "You'll be delighted, I have decided to go on the list." She wanted "to keep up with my baby boy in the park". Like me, she was now fully oxygen dependent and breathless walking.

Getting onto a transplant waiting list takes time. Tests are done. Medically a person must be considered sick enough to need one, and capable of surviving it. Sadly, Marie's health deteriorated swiftly as she was about to be placed on the list. She never got the chance to rear and run after her little boy. I often think about the beautiful soul she was, and the laughs we shared as we endured yet another hospital admission.

Almost three years after being put on the English transplant list, I was in hospital, desperately hoping for a call. Newcastle had always done Irish transplants for people with CF. I felt my better chance lay with them. The Irish lung transplant programme got up and running only in 2007. However, life takes you in directions you never imagined. The unexpected often comes to pass.

The danger was that, if I got called over to Newcastle, and the transplant did not go ahead, I might not be flown back to Dublin as I was perilously ill. I did not want to end my days in an unfamiliar setting. Something was telling me I needed to be on the Irish list. My inner voice directed me towards it.

Towards the end of June Ms Karen Redmond, an Irish lung transplant surgeon, called into St Vincent's to see about moving me onto the Irish list. "I need to get this transplant within the next few months," I said. Aghast, she replied, "You need to get it within the next few weeks."

People who are very ill don't actually realise how sick they are. I certainly did not fully absorb my situation. Maybe that was a blessing as, otherwise, I might not have persisted through the worst of it.

Karen put me on the Irish list the next day. One week later the call came. As I was wheeled into the operating theatre in the Mater Hospital, I felt a bizarre mix of terror and relief. There was nowhere else to go. This was the path I must travel for survival and a brighter future.

During my time on the waiting list, somebody asked, "What do you do with yourself at home? Do you get bored"? I struggled to answer. Then I could not see it but, looking back, the answer is obvious. I was too sick. I simply did not have the energy to be bored.

The greatest blessing post-transplant is being able to breathe freely. No more oxygen, no BiPap, and no coughing or spluttering. Now I have buckets of energy. Transplant is rightly described as the gift of life. For me, it is the regifting of life, as what I had previously was decimated by illness. What my donor has given me – a future – is priceless.

Life has been hectic. My family brought me to visit New York last year. Not having been able to fly for seven years, it was marvellous to turn up at the airport and head off. As a fellow transplant pal exulted, "The shackles are off!"

Simple things matter. Last summer, out cycling and pedalling along, it hit me how wonderful it was to be able to do this. To fully appreciate the present, I need to keep reminding myself how limited I was. It is easy to forget.

I'm doing what I enjoy, including drama and musical productions. Going to the gym is becoming addictive. Last year I did a diploma in radio production, followed by working in my local radio newsroom. Currently I am in the throes of a one-year full time Masters in Journalism in DCU. This summer, my Master's work placement is in television with TV3, a hugely exciting opportunity. It is amazing to be capable of doing all this. Being able is what counts, and realising my full potential is how I honour my donor.

I frequently think about him, the hero of my story. He was a 32 year old guy in the full of his health. Little did he know, right up to his accidental death, that his story would end. Life is unfair and utterly transient. Before my transplant I felt totally cheated, and had no concept of gratitude. Now gratitude comes naturally. But for receiving those lungs, I know I'd be dead. It was Mother Teresa who aptly said, "Yesterday is gone, tomorrow has not yet come. We have only today. Let us begin."

If somebody had handed me a cheque for an unimaginable amount when I was dangerously ill, I'd have had to return it. What I needed, new lungs, no amount of money could buy.

My wish is that sharing my story in this 'Get Up and Go Heroes' book will inspire people to get up and go at living a life they desire. I also hope it will promote awareness of organ donation.

I've learned the importance of being happy in the here and now. Go with your heart. Ignore the naysayers. Life is all too short, and cannot be lived backwards. Your future starts now!

ABOUT THE AUTHOR
Moira Ní Ghallachóir

Moira helps small business owners and entrepreneurs to inspire their way to more clients, customers and profits without being pushy or salesy. They can have the increased profits they yearn for, by doing what they love, to fuel a life they love, even if they hate sales! Moira brings her inspired, dynamic and successful brand of business mentoring all over the world, to show other entrepreneurs a bigger vision for their own businesses, and a powerful, authentic path to inspire their way to more contacts, contracts, clients and profits. Moira hosts unique business retreats for women in her beloved Donegal 'gno le chroi'. For more, see mng.ie.

*"If you're serious about changing your life,
you'll find a way. If you're not,
you'll find an excuse."*
JEN SINCERO

Sliding Doors

MOIRA NÍ GHALLACHÓIR

Every now and then, when taking a break between client calls, booking international flights, or programming my next immersive business event, I pause to wonder, What if...? What if I hadn't taken that leap six years ago? Where would I be? What would I be doing? How would I feel? How much money would I be earning? How many lives would I be changing?

I sip coffee, lean against the handmade customised desk in my home office, and my mind travels back. Gazing out over the fields, I take in the stunning view of the West Donegal mountains I gaze at every day, and remember that moment when I jumped from one life into another. It reminds me of the movie 'Sliding Doors', the one starring Gwyneth Paltrow, where she alternates between two parallel universes that reveal, depending on whichever decision she makes, the different paths her life could take.

On paper, and on Facebook, I had a near perfect life at the beginning of the New Year in 2012. I lived in a great apartment in London. My life was hectic, packed to the rafters with friends, fun, incredible meals, socialising, weekends away and guest list parties. I devoured that city. My full-time office job, working at a non-profit organisation with young people in London, afforded me the means to live well, and so I enjoyed wardrobes filled with clothes, designer handbags and shoes to die for. My work was intense but also rewarding. I helped vulnerable young people to navigate their lives, and worked hard to prevent them from becoming homeless.

This ultra fast-paced city lifestyle, jetsetting, parties, and fashion shows, as well as a meaningful and well-paid job, surely added up to a perfect life? It seemed that I had done well, made a success of myself – job done. Back home in Ireland my parents were proud of me.

But deep in my soul, a lingering doubt questioned all this glitz and glamour. Between the busy and the brilliant, an uneasy honesty gave birth to a truth that wouldn't go away. It kept creeping up and whispering in my ear. It was weary and earnest. It said things like, "You're not really happy" and "There's more to life than this" and "There is something better, something more, somewhere else." I'd push it away, my hands over my ears, and get back to being busy. But the whisper stayed with me, and grew louder and louder and louder until I couldn't ignore it anymore.

I realised that I was stuck and needed inspiration. It was the weekend of my birthday and, although I had loads of plans with mates, totally spontaneously I jumped on the next Eurostar to Paris. Alone, armed with nothing but a notebook, a head full of questions, and a heart full of longing, this was the first major step I took to becoming a hero in my own life. Sometimes, whether in life or in business, you have to break away in order to break through. In such moments of freedom and adventure, inspiration often comes to visit.

I sat at a Parisian cafe, sipping café au lait and making lists – of jobs, of places to move to, of new possibilities. Nothing felt like what I needed, until I heard a small voice in the back of my mind whispering, but more brightly this time. "Donegal," it said. Inspiration had struck, and she was speaking in the unmistakable Irish lilt of my people.

I had grown up in this Northwest corner of Ireland, and, as soon as I could, I began travelling the world, building homes in Budapest, Madrid, and New York, before settling in London. Growing up, I couldn't wait to leave, and I had never entertained the thought of moving home. But here I found myself in cosmopolitan Paris, croissant crumbs on my journal, and the thought of going back to Ireland flooded me with a feeling of peace. Clearly, my heart was on board.

My mind raced with a hundred questions; "What the hell? How can this happen? What about a job? Where will I live?"

I returned to London after my Parisian adventure, and immediately gave notice at my nine-to-five job. I bought a small car and began to pack my life into it. Within a month I had moved. I said goodbye to the city, and my dumbfounded friends, and set off on the 11 hour drive to my Irish countryside home.

I remember that journey so well. Even though I didn't have any answers to the big question of what lay ahead for me, I was filled with an overwhelming sense of peace, excitement and freedom. And, as the hills of Donegal came into view, and I saw my mother waiting for me at the gate, my heart burst with happiness. I was home, and a new chapter was about to begin.

Today I earn a six-figure sum. I'm a business coach who works with entrepreneurs to build the thriving businesses they've always wanted but didn't think they could have. I share my story in hopes that something within it ignites something inside you, and that you use that inspiration to create the life you've always wanted.

Do you ever find yourself wondering what it would be like to live the life of your dreams? Do you feel there's something more – a life filled with passion, adventure and fulfillment, free from the worries of how to pay for it? Do you imagine a 'Sliding Doors' scenario where, somewhere in another dimension, you are living the life you were meant to live?

This is the life I now live. I'm my own boss. My business has not only transformed my life, but also the lives of my clients. I have contributed to the economy of my area. I quadrupled my income in the past three years, and am a sought-after speaker who travels internationally several times a year.

When I came home, I moved into my Grandmother's cottage and began to renovate it. I reconnected with old friends, and spent time soaking up the incredible, unique identity of this place I knew as home. It was inspiring, and I began to see potential around every corner. I was buzzing. This place is amazing, I thought. Yet, I also saw how under-appreciated obvious resources were. We were in the eye of the recession storm and, for many people, the outlook was bleak. Local entrepreneurs were struggling, businesses were closing, and many people were moving away in search of something new.

The small-town authenticity that made Donegal so special also made aspects of it feel stuck in time. The place had a slightly stale energy. I didn't see many tourists or visitors. For some reason, rather than putting me off, this inspired me. I decided to harness my excitement and enthusiasm for the good of my homeplace. I pledged to attract visitors to this stunning part of the planet by creating a new tourism-based business. My previous background in travel and sales gave me the practical skills I needed, and the landscape around me was the impetus. I wanted to grow a business that I loved and was passionate about. My mission was to rekindle local people's zeal for the place where they live, and to bring international travellers to the area for fresh, energizing experiences. I wanted to inspire others to rediscover enthusiasm in their own lives just as I had. And I wanted to create incredible, heart-led adventures that supported local business owners and breathed vitality and vigour into the area.

I got a mixed response when I took my message to the streets. Some locals were doubtful, resigned to the way things were. A lot of people asked why I even bothered trying. "Why don't you just find a job?" people asked. Then there was the ever-popular, "What happens if it doesn't work?" I ignored all the doubt and scepticism and stuck to my intuition which told me to keep going.

I had ultimate faith that I could tap into the power of inspiration to exponentially grow my sales, attract clients, and ultimately, grow a thriving business – and that is exactly what happened. My excitement and encouragement drew in more and more business. In only three short years, my actions brought over one thousand visitors to Donegal.

When other businesses saw how successful I was, they started to ask for my help to grow theirs. I started coaching one, then another, and this just took off. I've gone from booking tours to leading retreats, and coaching business owners worldwide on how to grow their businesses through inspiration-based sales, as well as quadrupling my income. I speak at workshops and events in Ireland, England, and the US. I hold retreats that are designed to empower entrepreneurs. I'm now gearing up for my latest offer, an all-island speaking tour called 'Waking The Giants'.

The best part of this story is that my success is not unique. When you use inspiration as your fuel, anything is possible. I have supported numerous entrepreneurs in achieving similar levels of success. It is my privilege to empower them to create thriving businesses and lives they love, not through being pushy or salesy, but by naturally inspiring people.

The key to all this is not a complicated formula. Creating your business, and the life of your dreams, emanates from what you're already good at. Honestly, this makes your heart sing!

If you want to re-imagine a better life, here's a gift from me. It's a downloadable guide that reveals the secrets I used to change my life. Use it to transform your business and life in 30 days or less. You'll find it at www.mng.ie. You are also welcome to contact me personally if you need help with your business.

Finding clients by inspiring people is the most personally gratifying and surefire formula to grow your business. In sharing this story, my hope is that you incorporate the principle of "sales through inspiration" to build your own business and then live the deeply fulfilling life you've always dreamt of. Now that is something to aspire to!

ABOUT THE AUTHOR
Bill Liao

Bill Liao is an Australian entrepreneur, author, speaker and social networking pioneer now living in Cork with his wife and three children, and is engaged in not-for-profit work. A European venture partner with SOS Ventures, he specialises in startup accelerator programmes, especially internet and social media. He is co-founder and mentor at CoderDojo, a not-for-profit organisation that teaches children how to code. Launched in Ireland in mid-2011, it is now a worldwide movement. He has participated in 'The Hunger Project' in Uganda, New York and Mexico. He is a regular speaker and attendee at TED conferences and attends the World Economic Forum.

"A problem is simply a fact someone is resisting."
BILL LIAO

The Author Learns How to Make Soup

BILL LIAO

We all want to live a rich, rewarding and successful life – whatever "success" means – and a life we love. We are driven by the idea of mastery, yet often satisfied by daydreams. Instead of committing to something new, and giving it our all, we often end up not doing our best for ourselves, our family and community, and the world that we all share.

Growing up in the 1970s and '80s, I was a bullied, Chinese-Australian computer nerd and high-school dropout. Apart from basic short-term needs I drifted, frustrated rather than inspired, unsure of what to do, yet sensing that there was a lot to get excited about. I had a succession of low-paid, unsatisfying jobs. I wanted to achieve things, although I didn't even know where to start.

My very first job at 17 was with a former student of my mother's, who liked my enthusiasm for technology. In that start-up company I learned a lot about how people react under pressure, and what customers do, and how to stay curious. I saw that, by working extremely hard, people can start their own company , as long as they are prepared to fail, pick themselves up and go again.

Then I worked for Canon, the Japanese multinational, and learned about the corporate ladder, and the political games that people master in order to succeed in a corporate environment. I saw how comfortable and safe a corporate job can be, and how soul-destroying the environment is for anyone who dreams of something imaginative and meaningful. And I also came to appreciate the regular pay-check and company car.

The people who thwarted my itch to do something different in the tech area, made more money than me, and were in sales. However, working in one's own start-up nonprofit or profit business is a great deal more challenging than fitting into a niche in an already established company, as well being intellectually and emotionally, rather than financially, rewarding.

My darling wife Kerrie and I completed the Landmark Forum, a three-day course originally developed in the United States in the early 1970s by the controversial philosopher Werner Erhard. I had never heard of the Landmark Forum or Werner Erhard, and would never have taken the course were it not for a good friend's insistence. And I had no idea what to expect. Not only did I lack confidence, I also, after reading lots about it, had many doubts as to Landmark's legitimacy, So, deeply suspicious, in I went with my own water bottle, determined to be a critical eye. Despite those initial misgivings, I now know Werner to be an exceptionally direct and compassionate person, and a man of great insight.

At the end of the course, I declared that if what I had unlocked in myself was at all true, I would be a millionaire by the time I reached 30. And, while I got many practical tips, such as that asking the right questions is often better than having the right answers, the core of what I got was seeing that I could create my future from a vision of the future, rather than recreating the past.

"Your life works to the degree you keep your agreements."
WERNER ERHARD

Kerrie went to meet a woman named Lolita, then the Country Director for The Hunger Project in India. The Hunger Project, of which Werner Erhard was one of the founders, is an organisation dedicated to ending world hunger in Africa, Asia and Latin America. It empowers people to be self-reliant, meeting their own needs and creating a better future for their children. The techniques used inspire people – in this case women – to become agents of change in their communities, supporting community level projects, in tandem with local government.

Rather than being given hand-outs, a handshake engages them as partners. "They" becomes "we". The knowledge they already possess, and their understanding of the challenges they face, are strengths. They then realise what they are capable of, and maximise their potential by keeping their end of the bargain through the fulfilment of obligations.

"The most effective way to achieve right relations with any living thing is to look for the best in it, and then help that best into the fullest expression"
ALLEN J BOONE

Lolita made a request that has probably had a bigger impact on my life and work than anything else I have ever been asked. Not only did she want me to support a pledge that Kerrie had made that first evening, and which we could not afford, but also to pledge far more money than I had, or imagined I'd ever have, to the Hunger Project.

Because Lolita is a great communicator and so compelling, I really wanted to do what she suggested, and yet, as Kerrie and I had many more debts than assets, the prospect made me quite nervous. "Bill," she asked, "who would you have to become to be able to pay $50,000 to The Hunger Project without any suffering for yourself?"

Wow! That was a big question. I would have to become someone pretty special to do that. Already disconcerted, when I found out that Kerrie had already pledged $5,000, suddenly I wanted to be that sort of person. I made the pledge although, on paper, there was no obvious way for me to meet it.

After I made the pledge, I longed to feel confident and assured, but doubts assaulted me. Who did I think I was? Where was someone like me going to find $50,000 to spare? The image I summoned of who I would have to become was of somebody very different to me, someone far wiser, more assured and confident, and, possibly, a little taller and more stylishly dressed. In my mind's eye, this person did not wear thick plastic glasses.

I made my way to a small bookstore on the corner of a dark street and browsed through the business section. While there were a lot of great books, some of which I had already read, the most valuable lessons I had been given in business and life did not come from books. Rather they were encapsulated in a folktale that my Scottish grandmother used to tell when I was a little boy, the well known folktale of 'Stone Soup,' – where a magician or soldier persuades poor local people who individually refused them food to each add an ingredient to their 'stone' and water soup, which is then shared. A similar story pops up in many traditions around the world.

Soon after, I quit my 'good' job and started my first real business as an independent coach, working particularly with engineering companies to improve their sales. It was a leap of faith as well as a leap into the void. I tossed my first stone into an empty pot looking for others to contribute to our mutual success. By learning to listen to others, and enrolling them in my business, I had my first real success before the deadline on my pledge to Lolita. I had actually invested $100,000 in the Hunger Project, twice what I promised, and I had designed a purpose for myself – "Who I am is a world that works for all living things" – that still defines me.

In my business I communicated with others in a deeper, more meaningful way than in the past so that others felt heard. Living up to my promise to the Hunger Project showed that I was already capable of most of what I aspired to. By the time I had turned 31, I had become a millionaire several times over.

Many elements made all this possible. None of them are beyond the reach of anyone who is capable of honouring their word, declaring something as possible, and then taking actions consistent with getting from their starting point A to their target point Z by when they said they would.

By articulating your vision of this future, you gather people around you who, because they're inspired, contribute. The metaphorical stone is a brilliant expression of this. You cannot have a movement without first moving people with your story.

Since those successes, I have co-founded not one but two "Unicorns" with billion dollar market capitalisations. I have also co-founded WeForest.org, which is ending poverty and climate change by planting millions of trees and empowering local women, and CoderDojo, which allows the world's children to learn to programme computers completely free of charge. I am one of the biggest investors in female startups in the world, that make a 32% net return on investors' money. On top of all that I am still just a guy who lives a life I love with my family. My proudest achievement is my three great kids who are engaging in adventures of their own.

ABOUT THE AUTHOR
Nikki Bradley

Nikki Bradley is a speaker, client account manager, columnist, and fitness enthusiast, with a passion for adapted training. Diagnosed with a rare form of bone cancer at 16, she received a second total right hip replacement at the age of 26. Nikki founded a fitness-based awareness campaign called 'Fighting Fit For Ewing's' where she regularly participates in extreme physical challenges on crutches to highlight the importance of exercise for rehabilitation, and uses the national and international media coverage her story attracts to share her message with a wider audience. For more, see nikkibradleyspeaks.com.

*"A lazy person is an unhappy person.
The more you do, the better you will feel.
Trust me on that."*
NIKKI BRADLEY

When Life Gives You Lemons

NIKKI BRADLEY

Does exercise really help your head? Four years ago I would have given a non-committal shrug when addressing this question, and I couldn't have answered properly as I genuinely didn't know. Now, when responding to it, I would all but shout, 'Yes!!!' You might wonder what gives me the authority to answer with such passion? Let me explain.

My name is Nikki Bradley. I am 31 years old and live in wet and wonderful Donegal. I am also the founder of an awareness campaign called 'Fighting Fit For Ewing's', and a permanent crutch user.

Since 2003 I have been dealing with the aftermath of cancer where radiotherapy destroyed my right hip. Having had two total right hip replacements, a broken femur, a massive hip infection, a leg length discrepancy of 11cm, severe nerve and muscle damage and, most recently, learning that I am likely to lose my right leg, has changed me as a person. Where once I would have approached exercise with trepidation and little commitment, now I look forward to my regular training sessions and love the fact that I am physically strong.

In 2013, when I attended what I thought would be a run of the mill meeting with my consultant in St Vincent's Hospital, Dublin, my life changed. It was summer. I had spent the first half of the year having trial treatments, including nerve blocks, spinal cord stimulation and an epidural. All had failed miserably. I walked into the meeting with little enthusiasm, expecting my doctor to suggest another treatment. He sat me down and, with regret, informed me that we had reached the end of the road. The various teams – oncology, pain management and orthopaedic – had done everything possible, but they were officially stumped. My case was too unusual. In a nutshell, they were giving up on me. In addition, I was also told that I would remain on crutches for the rest of my life.

That meeting changed my life and my way of thinking. I walked out and wandered over to a wall where I sat for ages. I closed my eyes, tilting my head up to the sun, and felt the heat on my face. Anyone seeing me might have imagined that I didn't have a care in the world. While there I experienced something I hadn't felt in a long time, absolute freedom. In that moment I realised that I had put my life on hold while waiting to 'get better'. To be told I was not going to get better, that, in fact, I was likely to deteriorate further was, strangely, what I needed to hear.

Does Exercise Really Help Your Head?

Three weeks later my awareness campaign, 'Fighting Fit For Ewing's', was born. I set it up for two main reasons, to raise awareness of Ewing's Sarcoma, a rare form of bone cancer that had affected me in my teens, and to highlight the importance of exercise for rehabilitation.

I began to train regularly in the gym, lifting weights and pushing myself further than I had done before. Three months on, I was off all pain medication bar one. It may sound dramatic to say that simple exercise allowed me to stop medication that I had previously relied heavily on, but it is true. I was still in pain, but I was learning to get on with life regardless. I left each training session sore, tired and happy. Physically I was exhausted, but my mind was loving every minute. It's well known that exercise releases endorphins, so there was a reasonable explanation for my happiness, but it was more than that. I had an excellent trainer who pushed me. He knew that I was capable of more than I knew myself and, with his help, I became a different person. My attitude to everything changed. I was no longer afraid, which gave me a freedom I had not previously known. Six months on, I was physically and mentally stronger.

At times I struggled with my own thoughts, doubts and fears. I would lie awake at night worrying about genuinely scary things such as; 'Will I live to see 50?' or 'Am I strong enough to continue with the life I have been given?' I was scared and felt very isolated at times. After my initial diagnosis, when I resolved to speak with a professional, I felt almost ashamed that I wasn't strong enough to deal with my situation alone.

Pushing the boundaries physically allowed me to do something similar mentally. I talk openly about the importance of seeking professional help if needed, and I am proud of myself for taking that initial step all of those years ago. I have consulted numerous people many times over the years and will continue to do so if necessary, but I don't focus on the negative anymore. Thanks to my training, I have learned to be the kind of person who can enjoy life while dealing with serious physical pain and disability. Pain is not the deciding factor anymore. Where once I would have turned down an invitation because I was sore, I now accept regardless. I have a choice, and the pain will be there whether I sit on the couch or climb a mountain.

I decided to incorporate physical challenges into my campaign quite early on as I wanted to give example to others, the mantra being 'If she can do it then so can I!' I have climbed numerous mountains, some completely snow covered, I have abseiled into a 45ft high ice cave, scaled a glacier in Iceland, attempted a Guinness World Record in Holland, and became the first woman to abseil off Fanad Head Lighthouse in Co Donegal. In addition, I have completed numerous 5km races, swam 60 lengths of a swimming pool, climbed a 147ft sea stack, and successfully completed the Winter Edition Fan Dance, all while relying heavily on crutches.

The Fan Dance is a 24km trek across the Brecon Beacons in Wales, a march usually reserved for the British Special Forces. I completed it during severe winter conditions in approximately seven hours and 20 minutes. It was by far my toughest challenge but one I will never forget. There were moments where I felt unsure as to whether I could continue, and I was exhausted both mentally and physically when I finally crossed the finish line, but I was almost drunk with pride. It got me to appreciate what the human body is capable of and opened up a whole new world of adventure.

I met with consultants in Birmingham last year who worked with engineers to build a prosthesis that would restore some of my leg length and, in turn, improve my balance. I was warned from the beginning that the risk of infection with this surgery would be 50%. If the prosthesis became infected, it would be removed immediately, and I would be fast tracked to an inevitable full leg amputation. I also had the option to stay as I am, experiencing daily pain and huge discomfort as my already damaged hip deteriorates further. Not great options you will agree. It is a lot for one person to deal with. After much deliberation, I declined the offer of surgery. It was simply too big a risk to take.

I do not know what my future holds. Certainly I will endure more hardship, and I will continue my search for adventure. My mind has to be fed, and exercise is my food of choice. If I could give you one piece of advice it would be to try it for yourself. Don't just take my word for it. Get up and go!

ABOUT THE AUTHOR

Mai Hernon McEvilley

Born in Gurteen, Co Sligo, Mai's early career as a set-dancer was ended by a back injury. At a summer school given by Colm O'Donnell, she discovered her singing voice. She has recorded four CDs, toured England, Ireland, Europe, and America, performing and teaching at many big festivals. Now living in the greater Cincinnati area, she is a founding member of "Beeswing" and "Trí Scéalta" She founded "Secret Ireland Tours LLC" for small tours. She also produced and presented "Out and About USA" for Irish TV. For more, see www.maihernonirishtradsinger.com and www.SecretIrelandToursLLC.com.

*"Now, when something presents itself to me,
I am not afraid and grab it with both hands.
It will be either a lesson or a gift."*
MAI HERNON MCEVILLEY

Listen To The Universe

MAI HERNON MCEVILLEY

I hail from a small village called Gurteen in south Sligo, where there was nothing but traditional music, song and dance. This culture was all around me. I was soaked in it.

My mother died when she was 39, leaving six girls. I was one of the middle ones, nearly nine years old. Life was not easy. I got married when I was 21, and we had three wonderful boys. We were married for 20 years before we split up.

As a young child, my father would bring me to sessions where the older people would invite me to join a group dance. I would listen to great musicians playing reels and jigs and would delight in the songs that people sang. These songs and that music were in my head. I danced to my heart's content at céilís in the local parish hall and became a good dancer.

I would sing to myself but never let anybody hear me. One night, when I was singing to one of my children, my then husband's musical partner heard me and complimented my singing. I was very defensive, saying, "I don't sing". It was something I did for my own enjoyment. I raised the boys and worked at all sorts of jobs, from factories to office work to shops. I hated every one.

Every year I would so look forward to the local summer school in a nearby town, where I would settle my kids into their respective music classes. And then I would attend the set dancing classes until, in 1995, I ruptured a disc in my back just six weeks before the summer school and had an operation that stopped me from participating in the dancing. It nearly broke my heart as my kids joined their music classes and I had to stay outside the dancing class venue. It would have killed me to go in and just sit there and watch, and going home was not an option either. It felt as if my world had come to an end.

My mind went crazy, and then, out of nowhere, a voice in my head started whispering to go to the singing class. No I could not. I can't sing. They would all laugh at me. Go, go, just go, the voice insisted. I walked around the school three times, and it took about ten minutes before I could knock on the door of the classroom. Eventually I walked through that door into a whole new world, a world I never imagined I would experience, a world I never thought I could have.

The teacher that year was the man who had heard me sing to one of my kids years before. As soon as I came in, he said that it was about time, and he wanted me to sing for the class. I nearly died. This would be the very first time I ever sang in front of a group. Even though I did not realise it, that was the beginning of the life I have now. Three years later I was teaching that class, and the following year I recorded my first CD.

At this stage I had separated from my husband. I had the kids and was still working, but now I was being asked to perform at some venues, and my CD was being played on radio stations. In 2003 I was working three jobs. I had a mortgage, and three boys in college, and I was doing it all on my own. I was dreaming about the possibility of being in the music business full-time, but could not see any way of doing this, and I became very depressed.

A man in Cincinnati, who had heard a track of my CD, emailed me wanting to buy it. I forgot to answer and, about two months later, I got another email explaining the trouble he went to trying to contact me. I felt bad and sent him a CD with a long handwritten letter telling him about my culture, the village, my kids and their musical abilities. He told me about a book he was writing. Now and again he would contact me and ask how we in Ireland might say something.

One day he sent an email asking if I knew anyone who would proof read his draft, so I put him in touch with a best-selling author I knew, and forgot about it. By then, I had given up one of the jobs as I could not keep up that pace.

In May the boys finished their semester at college for the holidays. The two younger boys said that they did not want to return as they had no interest in college. I did not argue as I felt relieved.

Some of the pressure had lifted. At the end of May I found myself unemployed. I had enough money to pay the June mortgage, but had no idea what I was going to do for July. I prayed.

One day a letter arrived with a cheque in dollars, from the man from Cincinnati, telling me that my introduction to my best-selling author friend had changed his life, and he wanted to thank me. I could not believe it. When I changed the cheque into pounds it covered, to the penny, the mortgage for July. Well, I got another job before July was over, and things settled down a bit, but I was still depressed, so I prayed.

I heard about this woman who does energy healing and decided that I could not lose anything by going to her. Like the singing class years before, I had no idea how this would change my life. Slowly I started to feel better. I wanted to learn from her about energy healing. She taught me that and much more. I began to see everything in a different light. The depression lifted, and I was happier. I realised that if I wanted something, I had to believe I deserved it, and I also knew that I had to make it happen.

I met the man from Cincinnati, and we became friends. A year later he came back, and we started a relationship. Long-distance relationships are not easy. I would get gigs at festivals in Ireland and England, but this was not a regular thing. I changed jobs a few times. At this stage, I was living on my own with my two dogs out in the country and working at a job that was paying the bills. The job was great until the management changed and, very quickly, things deteriorated. I was bullied and treated badly, to the point where I lost patches of my hair. I had forgotten all I learned about energy and listening to God and the universe. The guy from Cincinnati never gave up. He would send an occasional text telling me how much he loved me, and ring me now and again. He asked me to marry him and move over to the States.

One evening someone sent a text telling me that a mutual friend aged 55 had died all of a sudden. It was like a light went on in my head. I had not been listening, I had not been heeding the signs. Suddenly I saw that my back injury had led me to singing, which led to making a CD, which led to me meeting Mick, the Cincinnati guy, who was asking me to go to America. We would go on the road together performing – I forgot to mention that he is a great singer and guitar player. As I was not listening, either the universe or, as I like to think, God decided to make my job difficult, so that I would see where I was supposed to be. I listened, became aware, and acted. It was my 'Get up and go' moment.

Now I perform all around America and teach traditional singing and dance. I have four CDs and am working on number five. I set up my own small group tour business, and even got the opportunity to produce and present my own TV programme. I am happily married to Mick. This all started because I was afraid of going into that singing class and went anyway. Now, when something presents itself to me, I am not afraid and grab it with both hands. It will be either a lesson or a gift. If you don't get up and go, you will never discover if you can make it.

ABOUT THE AUTHOR

George Hillen

George Hillen is an Irishman and a police officer in the Northern Territory of Australia where he lives with his wife Veronica, daughter Isobel and his sidekick Mac the dog. After experiencing a diagnosis of the most deadly of adult cancers, George made a few promises which he didn't think he would be fortunate enough to keep. But he was, and he did! Pancreatic cancer has a five year survival rate of under 8% and the treatment is harsh. Surgery removed most of George's stomach, pancreas and upper intestine followed by six months of chemotherapy. Two and a half years after surgery George climbed Kilimanjaro, the tallest mountain in Africa and raised more than $130,000 for awareness and research into the disease. A year later Isobel was born.

""On 23 July, Sally Ride, the first female astronaut, died of pancreatic cancer. If I survived, I swore I would tell some of my story."

GEORGE HILLEN

Life Interrupted

GEORGE HILLEN

I came from Ireland to Australia in February 1996 on a working holiday, landed in Sydney and fell in love with the place. Now I live and work in Katherine as a police officer in the Northern Territory. This district covers one of the largest geographical policing areas in the world. I have private health insurance.

2012 was an intense, difficult year. It kicked off with my sister having a baby, due on the seventeenth of March, on New Year's Eve. I came close to getting on a plane and going home. In May of that year I woke at two in the morning with severe stomach cramps. I weathered them and went back to bed. Next day, feeling tired, I went to Darwin with my boss for the sentencing of a guy found guilty of supplying drugs in remote communities. Two nights later, I had cramps again. My partner Veronica came with me to the local accident and emergency department. A young doctor told me it might be gall stones. They gave me pain relief. After an ultrasound I arranged to go to Darwin the next morning. Pancreatitis was mentioned. Released from hospital after a day or two, I called my mum and told her I had been a bit sick but was okay.

The following week I had an appointment with the surgeon in Darwin. He suggested putting a camera down my throat to see what was causing the problem. A gall stone might have lodged somewhere. He warned me about the risk of cancer, but I was dismissive. I was keeping on top of my fitness at the RAAF gym at the base close to Katherine at least three times a week. I connected losing 15 kilos in weight to an improved diet and training hard.

The surgeon found no gall stones. There was something that could be cancer. I told a couple of people, and continued to go to the gym with my work partner Luke. I asked Luke to ask his Mum, Ann, an experienced nurse, a few things. What sticks in my mind was, "Pancreatic Cancer is the cancer you don't want to get."

I knew I had a pancreas that produces insulin, but that was it. I decided not to check the internet, and to listen to what the doctors said. I made a will and left everything to Veronica. I said a Novena to Saint Jude, the patron saint of lost causes.

My decision not to tell my family turned out to be a lot harder than I imagined. If my mum found out, she would have been on the first plane out. She'd been ill. I was worried about the toll on her.

Keeping the news of pancreatic cancer from your family is not easy. I asked my bosses, and colleagues and friends who knew, not to tell anyone. There are lots of Irish in Australia, and quite a few from my home town. And news travels fast, especially news about cancer.

A tumor the size of an olive had interrupted the function of my liver and that's why I was jaundiced. I would have to travel to Adelaide to have surgery. Veronica was sitting next to me when the surgeon in Darwin explained the "Whipple's Procedure".

Veronica and I had planned on moving back to Darwin. We put a deposit on a four-bedroom house in an outer suburb with room for our dogs to chase balls. Because of what was happening, we pulled out of the house and land package and lost about $3,500.

We travelled to Adelaide where I had a biopsy. The surgeon explained how the pancreas was attached to a blood vessel, that the plumbing between the liver and the stomach is complicated. They would have to remove a large portion of my stomach, a section of the bowel and part of the pancreas itself. The "Whipple's" was scheduled for 29 June 2012.

The surgeon phoned to say the biopsy had come back negative. And another biopsy came back negative. I was waiting for the doctors to say, "Sorry George, we stuffed up! You're fine!"

Despite the negative biopsies, there was something there. The surgeon and I decided to continue with the operation two weeks later. As we left his office, Veronica and I realised that surgery was scheduled for Friday 13. I had become superstitious.

We flew to Darwin and drove to Katherine to spend a week at home with our dogs, Mac and Scent. Around this time I found out that my brother in Ireland was having heart problems and had a stent put in. I got word that my mum had a checkup, and had been kept in hospital with an elevated heart rate because of a thyroid problem. I would not have forgiven myself if I had said anything that made things worse. It felt like I was being punished, like my family was being punished. I got really angry.

I went to the hospital in Adelaide on the Friday morning where I was prepped and brought to the theatre. On the Sunday I awoke, intubated. I had been anaesthetised with pethidine, also an epidural that didn't work, and I had ketamine.

I had drain tubes into my left and right sides, and – what I had feared – a catheter going into my bladder. My stomach was stapled. It looked like I was attacked by a shark. I have vivid memories of a visit from the surgeon in the High Dependency Unit. He told me that it was cancer and that the margins were clear.

After a few more days in HDU I was moved to a ward. I called my Mum and told her I was on a bush trip connected with work and mightn't be contactable. I would call her when I got back.

Veronica would stay all day. I saw the toll this was taking on her. I realised that my decision to keep this secret was hard on the people I confided in. They couldn't vent.

After surgery the remainder of the stomach – the remnant – wouldn't work. Eventually it would, but they didn't know when. I had to keep eating, and my stomach was drained through a tube from my nose to it, until it started working mid-August. I used to love when Veronica got me a small tub of tasty mash and gravy from the KFC across the road. It came back up easy. And, if I never have jelly again, I don't care.

Lying in the hospital bed in Adelaide, shortly after the "Whipple's Procedure", I started to look on the internet for stories of Pancreatic Cancer survival. The average survival rate for someone diagnosed with Pancreatic Cancer is three to six months. Only 15-20% of those diagnosed are able to undergo a "Whipple's" and, of those, only about 15% are expected to have a five-year survival. I was angry, scared and frustrated.

For a long time I didn't find survivor stories because they were swamped by the stories of those who didn't, Patrick Swayze and Steve Jobs. Chris Rea did, and I found some comfort in that. On 23 July, Sally Ride, the first female astronaut, died of pancreatic cancer. If I survived, I swore I would tell some of my story.

I went for a walk with all my tubes and staples. Rolling an intravenous drip stand along, I passed the Intensive Care and High Dependency Units. Every step was laboured but necessary to get a plan in my head for recovery. Afterwards, I was more exhausted and in more pain than ever before in my life.

Four promises I made then included visiting my family in Ireland and telling them about my illness. This motivated me to eat and exercise during the six months of chemotherapy. I wanted to appear healthy. The second was that I would get married to my now wife Veronica, and the third was a collaboration with Luke. He suggested travelling to Africa, to climb Mount Kilimanjaro, the highest freestanding mountain in the world. The fourth I kept to myself.

From 105 kilos six months before the operation, I was down to 74. The cancer counsellor talked about fighting cancer. What do you do, stand on the street and shake your fists at the sky? We spoke about choosing songs for my funeral. I left hospital and flew to Darwin with a tube in my nose. The in-flight movies were about Eddie Mabo and Steve Jobs, not survivor stories. When we landed, Veronica drove to Katherine, returning the next morning with Mac and Scent. I was allowed out of hospital for a few hours. In Luke's house I got an uplifting welcome from the dogs. The next day the nasal-gastric tube was removed, and I was allowed home.

The oncologist in Darwin at the Alan Walker Cancer Centre gave me the whole chemo induction. The Friday drive back from chemotherapy to Katherine from Darwin took longer than the outward journey because of the danger of hitting wallabies at dusk. The nurses were gold. I'd go back to say hello and thank you but I don't want to set foot there again. Before chemo, a test revealed that I have latent tuberculosis, but I didn't receive treatment because of reduced liver function.

When Big Steve, my great buddy from working in pubs in Darwin years ago was having a few beers, he would say, "The liver is evil. It must be punished." A few weeks into chemo, I saw Big Steve coming out of the chemo suite. He was there with his mother. When he saw my wristband, and I came clean, his face changed. I felt a dickhead for not telling him. I won't expand on chemo. It is what it is. If I hadn't my dogs as company when Veronica was at work I would have gone crazy. Afterwards, my scan was clear.

In 2013 I spent a fantastic five weeks with family and friends in Ireland. My mum wasn't happy she wasn't told. In 2014, Veronica and I spent a month there before getting married in a castle on the rugged coast of Co Down, near where I grew up.

On 27 February 2015, with our friend Paul Lawson, Luke and I reached the summit of Mount Kilimanjaro. Supported by The Northern Territory Police, Government, and branch of the Australian Hotels' Association, we raised $131,727.84 for Avner's Foundation for research into pancreatic cancer.

On our return from Africa, Luke and his partner Kerry had fantastic news. They were expecting their first child. Veronica and I soon had a similar announcement. Five weeks after Luke's son Eli was born in September, my fourth promise was realised when we welcomed a beautiful daughter into the world, Isobel Jude Grace Hillen.

I'm back working. I don't know what the next few years will hold, but I'll give Isobel the best start in life, and I'll be looking for challenges to raise awareness of pancreatic cancer.

ABOUT THE AUTHOR

Fearghal O Nualláin

Fearghal is fuelled by a curiosity about the limits of his comfort zone, and new ways of learning about the people, places and environments that make up our world. Curiosity has driven him to complete the first Irish circumnavigation of the Globe by bike; a 31,000km 18-month cycle around the planet through some of the highest, driest, poorest and hottest places on earth and walk across Rwanda to research a thesis in environment and development. He has entertained, informed, and motivated audiences of ten to a 1,000 with stories from over ten years of human powered adventures great and small. He's currently travelling the Indus river by human power to make a documentary about water. See www. fearghalo.com to follow Fearghal's Adventures.

"We shall not cease from exploration, and the end of all our exploring will be to arrive where we started and know the place for the first time."
TS ELIOT

Arrive Where We Started

FEARGHAL O NUALLÁIN

It's out there beyond the screen, beyond the front door, beyond the gate beyond the end of the road. A world full of experience.

The world teaches us much more than books ever can. In a time when we can zoom down to ground level anywhere in the world from the numb warmth of our desks, going can seem like an indulgence. In a time when false information about people and places can cloud the truth like a blizzard, the only way to know for sure is to see for yourself.

TS Eliot knew it. "We shall not cease from exploration," he said, "and the end of all our exploring will be to arrive where we started and know the place for the first time." He knew that the need to satisfy the urge to "get up and go" is hardwired into us all. Scratch the itch.

It is almost ten years since I embarked on a big journey to learn this lesson. In 2008 I packed all my worldly possessions into a trailer, hooked it up to a bike, hopped on that, and headed west. I spent 18 months cycling around the world to learn for myself a simple truth, I wanted to know that the world is round. A poor return on a hard year and a half's work, you might say. I could have flown around the world in a few days. Had I paid attention in school I would already have known for sure that the world was round. But would I truly have known? Can you ever be sure if you don't go? Seeing is, as they say, believing. So is smelling and feeling and hearing. Knowing is more than just figures and objective facts. At its most pure, it is an experience.

On this 31,000km cycling transect around this planet I propelled myself over mountain ranges, through cities and villages. The left side of my body was burned by the sun in the Taklamakan desert, and my breath froze to my beard in central Turkey. In Peru I gasped for breathe in the thin Andean air, in far western China I was grateful for the oxygen-rich air of one of the lowest points on earth. In Iran I was attacked by three men with knives, and I considered giving up, finishing the journey in the air conditioned safety of an airplane cabin. But, if I did, I knew I'd never forgive myself so I continued cycling in the direction that my attackers had fled.

A lap of the planet by bike is the best lesson a geographer could hope for. It provided a well rounded knowledge of the world that I could never hope to have gained from a book, it painted a richer picture than I could ever dream of on a high-res computer screen. It left me with desert sand in my hair, the burn of a thousand hills in my calves, and a taste for the lesser known parts of the four corners.

You'll never realise your potential unless you go and look for it. Going is difficult, it is scary. Leaving the cave takes an impetus, a drive, an urge, a reason. People will tell you to settle, and stay put. But don't pay any heed. Just go.

Nobody ever learned anything worth knowing by staying put. Exploring self and the world is arduous by nature. But with risks come returns and, only through hardships, comes strength. If you never go you'll never know how if you can keep your head while all around are losing theirs, or how big your heart and tough your sinew. You'll never know how far you could go, and what seeds your explorations might sow. What a loss that would be. Go, come back and tell your story to anyone who'll listen. The world needs that. Now more than ever. As traditional media fails and digital channels get choked with noise, we need old fashioned knowledge and hard won truths borne of experience.

Arriving in my hometown after powering myself around the world I was greeted with a familiar landscape but I saw it anew with fresh eyes. I returned with a new appreciation for the little things, a hot shower, a fridge, a warm bed. Too often we rely on second hand knowledge distorted by the inaccurate replication of multiple whispers. The world needs you to go, to explore and discover, and to come home "and know that place for the first time".

ABOUT THE AUTHOR

Gerry Duffy

Gerry Duffy is a professional speaker in the areas of goal-setting, personal development, motivation and leadership. He has been hired by over 500 companies and organisations including Facebook, Google, Bank of America, Novartis Pharmaceuticals and Coca Cola. He has a masters in business practice and has written three books including 'The Goal Getter' (2015). Since 2003, Gerry has run 32 marathons in 32 consecutive days, as well as completing and winning the inaugural Deca Enduroman UK Challenge – dubbed 'the toughest 10-day endurance challenge in the world' in 2011.

"If we have the courage to put ourselves forward for things, life becomes unrecognisable in terms of the happiness levels we reach."
GERRY DUFFY

The Dancer And The Dance

GERRY DUFFY

Recently I was working with an audience of over 350 people. During my presentation I asked them to stand up if they had ever been to a wedding. All stood up. Then I asked them to stay standing if they had danced at the wedding. Nobody moved.

"So you can dance," I said.

They realised that I had trapped them into telling me something they were able to do. It hardly mattered, until I informed them that, in less than two minutes, we would all be dancing. As that detail sank in, previous looks of comfort and relaxation on the faces of almost everyone vanished.

I asked them to tell me how they were now feeling. They confessed to anxiety, fear, self-consciousness, nervousness, embarrassment and apprehension. As they volunteered the words, I captured them on a flipchart in big red ink. Then we danced for ninety seconds.

Before they danced, I requested them to move with abandon, and as well as they were able. We did it and then all sat down. As they relaxed into their chairs, I asked them how they were feeling.

Everything they fed back to me – energised, happy, young again, enthused, fantastic, great fun – I wrote in a different colour on the opposite side of the flipchart page.

The point of all this was to question how much we hold ourselves back from what we are able to do. The dancing was just a metaphor for life. My audience were unmotivated to dance even though they knew they could. Yet look at what awaited them when they did get up and dance. So why do we hold back?

If I had begun by asking them who could dance, I predict that 50% would have told me they couldn't. But that would have been because of disinclination rather than ability. They had already told me that they could dance.

I stood back and invited them to let the stark contrast in the words on the flipchart sink in. On one side of the sheet was anxiousness. Immediately opposite was the word energised. Fear, embarrassed and nervous had been replaced with happy, fantastic and fun.

It begs the question of how much we talk ourselves out of what we can do, which, if we got out of our comfort zone, would be rewarding for us. What I've learned about life is that almost everything we want – energy, happiness, fun – lies beyond fear, apprehension and nervousness.

I want to encourage you to dance. For you, dance might represent giving up cigarettes, signing up for a night class, volunteering to sing on a stage, asking someone out on a date, taking up a new activity, moving somewhere new, losing weight, going for an even better job, pushing for a bigger contract, or opening a business.

You might say, "Well Gerry that's ok for you. You have no issue with it." Well, that's not actually true. Once upon a time I was invited to dance, but I was incredibly fearful.

Let me share my own dancing story. And I'll begin by sharing who I am now. I am a full time speaker and business trainer. Over the course of a year, I might address over 150 different audiences, ranging in size from three to 3,000 people. I've been fortunate to work in some amazing environments with some wonderful companies. I travel to many marvellous countries. I am passionate about speaking and training. In a typical year I might stand in front of 30,000 or more people. Every week I wake up at 5am so excited because I am going to spend the day working in the areas in which I have expertise with some corporate group. I love it.

This isn't the full story yet. Let me share who I was. Twelve years ago public speaking was the biggest fear of my life. In 2005 I was pathologically afraid of it, so fearful that I had to attend a hypnotist to help me to summon up the courage to address an audience of just four. Walking into that presentation back in September 2005, I wasn't just anxious, self-conscious or nervous. I was terrified. Now I understand that, if we have the courage to put ourselves forward for things, life becomes unrecognisable in terms of the happiness levels we reach. Confidence and higher levels of happiness do not just come from reading a book. They come from doing. As a consequence of what I do, I've become much more confident.

Having spoken to my audience of four in 2005, I had no ambition to speak professionally. It took every sinew of courage I possessed to stand up that day. I was relieved to have survived what felt like an ordeal. As a consequence of actually doing it, I got massive confidence. "What else have you been telling yourself you cannot do?" I asked myself many times in the weeks after.

At the time I had no further ambitions to speak publicly but then, four years later, when I was looking to identify a new career path, and searching for skills I could bring to the marketplace, I did. If I hadn't danced back in 2005, I would not have known that I possessed that new found skill. You can imagine how glad I was that I had given the talk. That's the other thing I got. Small keys can open big doors!

If, reading this, you see something in your life that causes fear, apprehension, or something you'd love to do but perhaps are a little scared of, I encourage you to stand up and dance. I am confident that what awaits you is more energy, fun and happiness.

ABOUT THE AUTHOR

Amy Waterman

Amy D Waterman PhD, is a social psychologist and professor at the University of California, Los Angeles (UCLA). While working at a transplant centre, she has heard many stories of kidney patients and living donors and been personally transformed by them. While solving the kidney donor shortage is her commitment, her work also illustrates the beauty of people becoming profoundly connected. She has published over 75 research articles, received $22 million in grants, started an educational nonprofit corporation, 'Explore Transplant', and worked within the United States, Canada, and Singapore to disseminate transplant education to tens of thousands of people.

*"Have only one rule, be your wild,
courageous brilliant self every single day,
no matter what."*
ANONYMOUS

The Same Colour Inside

AMY WATERMAN

That morning I got an email from the kidney surgeon. It was direct: "Transplant surgery tomorrow. Need permission from the family to observe. Meet me at 4pm," it said

I left my office and walked to the transplant centre. As I didn't know that I would be meeting patients beforehand, I hadn't dressed for the occasion. Where was my lab coat and badge? Instead, a glimpse of pale lavender tights peeked out between my floral skirt and brown boots. I felt like a kid caught wearing a pink tutu to school.

Twenty minutes later, the surgeon rounded the corner and gestured at me to come into a patient's room. I didn't really like this guy. Three years ago, he had yelled so loudly at me in this same hall that the nurses in the main bay couldn't look me in the eye afterward.

He had yelled because I was running a research study for potential living kidney donors. One of the questions was whether the donors wanted or needed any money to cover the costs of childcare, time off work, or lost wages. In the survey, I had asked them how much they needed.

"Those donors are going to think that we will pay them to donate! That's illegal." His words were a punch to the soft part of my stomach. He had challenged my research ethics as a psychologist. My eyes burned and I blinked to avoid tears. The elevator doors had opened and closed, and new patients arriving for their transplant appointments witnessed my pink face.

Be logical, rational, calm, I thought. "Sir," I said, "during the research study I told them that they wouldn't be offered money as part of receiving their healthcare here. And I got permission from the administrator of the transplant center."

"But you didn't ask me," was all he said.

That night I didn't sleep, wondering if my research and education programme would be shut down. A surgeon is the king of the transplant kingdom. If he complained, I might lose access to patients to conduct my research. My brain whirled. I wondered if I would have to leave the city or find another research topic. I stopped the study and never published anything about reimbursing donor costs.

Now he and I were together walking into room 1503. Near the door an older African-American woman sat in a bed, looking small and scared. A 20-something boy played a handheld video game in the bed beside the window. His extreme thinness registered immediately.

Two other men were in the room, one burly man sitting in a chair that looked too small for him, and another speaking to the woman. The surgeon explained that, the following day, the woman in the bed was donating her kidney to her son.

The doctor told the family that I was making a transplant video to help patients learn about their options. I asked the woman if it was okay to film their donation and surgery. Her husband standing beside her asked if I could send them a film copy of the two surgeries. I agreed.

The mom signed the permission forms without speaking. I smiled, trying to be reassuring. As I handed the son the clipboard to sign the paperwork, I wanted to pull him aside. I wanted to say that, with a transplant, he would have more freedom to get away from his parents. And stop feeling so sick. But he didn't look up. "The doctor is very good," was all I said.

As the surgeon and I walked down the hall, he told me that the big guy in the chair was a famous football player. He pulled out his phone to show me a picture someone had taken of the two of them earlier, the surgeon overshadowed by the footballer twice his size. I smiled as if I knew and cared who the footballer was, neither of which was true.

"I will see you at 6am tomorrow," he said, and we went our separate ways.

At 5am the next morning, I decided that observing kidney surgery was a bad idea. I never watch horror movies. I couldn't even remove a splinter my niece got climbing over a fence from her finger. It's not the blood. It's about too much empathy. If people aren't okay, if they are in pain, I worry too much. But the surgeon was expecting me, as was the videographer.

So, slightly nauseated, off I went. In the changing room, the videographer and I dressed in green scrubs and stood outside as the kidney patient was getting prepped for surgery. The mother's donation surgery had already started in the operating room next door.

Watching through a small window in the door, I started to feel very light-headed. "You aren't going to pass out on me, are you?" the surgeon had asked before agreeing to let us film the surgery. I promised that I wouldn't, but I began to regret that vow. The scrubs felt claustrophobic. I was woozy. I took deep breaths to calm myself.

The operating room doors swung open and, gloved and masked, the surgeon appeared. His short stature was comforting. He seemed less intimidating when I could see only an inch of his face.

The anesthesiologist sat by the boy's head monitoring his vital signs. Everyone took their position. Nurses rolled up metal instruments. The videographer filmed, I watched. Only a small area of the boy's abdomen was exposed – he could have been anyone.

I thought about what had happened in room 1503 that morning. I thought about the mom saying goodbye to her husband. I hoped she wasn't scared. I thought about the son and mother being wheeled on two gurneys into the operating room. Did they say goodbye? Against the wall in the surgical suite, wearing the equivalent of a shower cap, I started to pray for them and for success with the two operations, and for the doctor who had been so hard on me.

Someone turned on a radio and the song, "Heard it through the Grapevine," came on. The energy in the room was a little peppy, for 6am. I bent my knees up and down slightly, keeping time with the song. I could see what was happening at the incision site from a television screen above the patient.

The doctor asked for an instrument from a nurse. I expected a lot of blood, but he made the incision with an instrument that burned the edges of the wound as it cut, and stopped the blood vessels from bleeding. Then he used a little vacuum like the ones dentists use to suction out blood.

The videographer moved around capturing the action. I took pictures of the tray of instruments, and a group of green-robed healthcare professionals, their heads clustered together. The anesthesiologist reported vital signs. One nurse gave out instruments. They counted the number of sponges going in and coming out. The doctor gave instructions, a spelunker light affixed to his head. It illuminated the patient's body cavity when he looked down and lit up the wall when he looked up.

Another surgeon came in to tell us that the living donor's kidney was ready. The videographer and I went next door into the other operating room. The surgeon there carefully cut the veins and ureter from the donor's kidney and removed it. It was only the size of my fist.

The doctor put the kidney in a small bowl of ice and rinsed away all the blood. It was pink. After a few minutes, when the blood was rinsed away, it faded to white. I photographed it in the bowl of ice. I asked the doctor if everyone's organs look the same, no matter their race. "We are all the same colour inside," he said.

We returned to the first operating room. My surgeon took the white, chilled kidney out of the ice and sewed its vessels into the bladder. Slowly the kidney started filling up with blood.

Twenty minutes passed. "See, see," he said, gesturing to me over his shoulder, "come closer. It is getting pink. Now wait."

And we looked down together, shoulder to shoulder, sharing the sterile field. When the kidney started making urine, he said, "Her son now has a functioning kidney." He looked over with smiling brown eyes. My eyes were teary. I felt I was in love with this surgeon.

ABOUT THE AUTHOR

Pat Falvey

Pat Falvey is an explorer, entrepreneur, expedition leader, logistical strategist, author, film producer and international inspirational speaker. He started his first business at 15 years of age, and has since had businesses in property development, finance, construction, insurance, tourism and film production. He was the first person in the world to complete the Seven Summits challenge twice by reaching the summit of Mount Everest from both the Tibetan and the Nepalese sides. He has experienced booms, busts, successes and failures in both his business and adventure life. Over 30 years, he has worked with and led, thousands of people to achieve their personal, business and adventure goals. He believes we are all ordinary but that what we do makes us extraordinary. He was born in 1957 in Ireland and lives in Co Kerry. For more, see www.patfalvey.com

"Hold nothing back/learn to find ease in risk."
JOHN O'DONOHUE (A NEW BEGINNING)

Awaken Your Spirit

PAT FALVEY

For much of my life I have been an explorer, adventurer, and entrepreneur. I have travelled to the furthest regions of planet earth, and have had the honour of being in places that few other get to, seeing nature in all its pristine majesty and ferocity. For over 30 years, I have worked with and helped thousands of people to follow their dreams with conviction and passion, and to make their goal a reality. Personally, I have had spectacular successes and failures in life, and have learned many lessons along the way.

The most profound thing I now know is that the greatest exploration of all is the exploration of our mindset. What goes on in our minds colours our days and shapes our lives. We are what we think, and how we think. Therefore, it is vitally important to explore our mindset to see if it is our friend or enemy, either helping or preventing us from leading the life we want to lead. We are all capable of being extraordinary. What we do and think, and how we act, makes our lives extraordinary.

My own life has been a roller coaster. I was born into a family of bricklayers in a close-knit, working-class community on the northside of Cork City, Ireland. I too was destined to become a bricklayer, but my grandmother, and earliest mentor, Mary B, taught me at a young age that I could be and do anything I wanted. When I was six years old, I went to live with her and became her apprentice. By the time I was ten, I had my first business, collecting second hand clothes that Mary B would later sell at local markets.

With the self-belief she instilled in me, I left school at 15 to become a millionaire. I started work as a bricklayer, but soon moved into property development. I was young, hungry, and full of energy, and believed that the world was mine for the taking. By the time I was 23, I was living in my dream house, owned flashy cars, and was married with two young children. I worked hard, played hard and was ruthless. I was making more money than I believed possible and loved every minute. But life had hard lessons in store for me. The recession of the 1980s exposed all my weaknesses. I hadn't been looking at the bigger picture, and didn't see the downturn coming.

I took my eye off the ball and lost my businesses due to overtrading, selfishness and greed. My self esteem and confidence were at an all time low. I became depressed and tried to take my own life on 6 September 1986. I drove towards an open wharf at high speed. Moments from entering the water, an image of my young sons' faces appeared before me. I slammed on the brakes, and the car stopped just before the river. I wept at the Quayside.

I had no other dream, no other plan. I, who had believed I was invincible, was failing. I felt trapped and ashamed, and could no longer cope. But, in 1980s Ireland, nobody, especially a man, could admit such a thing. However, people close to me knew my situation and, while no one addressed my emotional distress, they did what they could to help.

One day, my secretary's father, an avid hillwalker, came to my office and insisted that I join his group the following Sunday for a hike. I had zero interest in or energy for such activity, but he wouldn't go away, and just to get rid of him I agreed. He still didn't go away and, on Sunday, when I felt I should be in my office worrying about everything, I found myself heading for the mountains of Kerry with a group of strangers.

I was way out of my comfort zone. I had to focus on each step I took, and my natural instinct to succeed kicked in. I was determined to reach the mountaintop. When I did, for the first time in a long time I felt I had succeeded at something. I liked that feeling and wanted it again. Energised by my first ever climb, and looking forward to the next one, I returned to Cork. That week, I was buzzing with new energy, and viewing my problems more positively, although I didn't know why.

The next week I climbed Carrauntuohill, Ireland's highest mountain, and felt alive. That Sunday I told my fellow climbers I was going to climb Mount Everest, the world's highest mountain. They thought I was mad. I didn't care. I was going to do it. Seven years later I stood on the summit of Everest for the first time.

After that, I became an explorer, visiting some of the most beautiful, remote and hostile parts of the planet. I climbed Everest four times, summiting twice. Jointly, I led the first Irish team to reach the South Pole, and the first Irish crossing of Greenland, while also leading over 80 exciting successful adventures throughout the world. I met people from almost every country, and learned that more unites us than divides us.

I returned to business life, older and wiser, bringing with me the lessons I had gleaned from my first big failure, and all that I had discovered while challenging myself to the limits of my capabilities, and exploring who I really was when travelling the world. The valuable lessons I learned during those years have become my guiding principles in life. The most important truth is that life is an adventure. The greatest exploration is engaging with our mindset in order to live our best possible life.

In my book 'You Have The Power', I outline the lessons I have learned throughout my business and adventure life, and the insights I have gained from the many people I encountered... and explore how to break free from the idea that there is only one version of yourself that you can be.

Many of us don't know what we want. We don't allow ourselves freedom to dream, and don't know what tools will enable us to dream in full colour. Early in life I learned that we should dream big, visualise our dreams as if they were already reality, and fuel that want with passion, ambition and self belief. Once we identify what we want, then we must take action. Without action, nothing happens, but many of us stop at this juncture.

Between dreaming and acting, it is important to formulate a goal, make a plan, and set a time-frame.

My years in formal education were not successful. The greatest knowledge I gained was outside school walls. The countries I travelled to, and the people I met, have made me a lifelong student. I am always on a learning continuum, from apprentice to master to apprentice. By being open, mastering new skills, getting out of your comfort zone, challenging yourself, making mistakes, getting to know your limits and moving beyond them, you can engage with the adventure of your life.

My mind and body were the engines that got me to the upper reaches of high-altitude mountains, and the farthest points of the poles. There was no back up, and no opportunity to take it easy. Throughout life, to give ourselves the best chance to succeed, we have to look after our mind and body, and be clear about what we stand for. We need to develop healthy networks, and to feed our body and mind healthy 'food', either actual food, or self-talk in our heads.

Becoming and remaining efficient helps us to achieve our goals. We need to ask if the rules we are living by are serving or limiting us, and to discover how to travel light physically and mentally. Baggage of all sorts weighs us down and impedes progress.

Clear communication is a key attribute of efficiency. We can't afford to make assumptions. Check and recheck that what you say is being heard, and that what you hear is what is being said.

Life is full of challenges, and how we negotiate them and our opportunities shapes our experience of life. Consequently we need to realise the importance of attitude in the daily choices we make. I have learned that choosing to be happy, grateful, humble and caring makes life easier. And laughter and celebration are as important as the air that we breathe.

One of the greatest challenges facing all of us is finding balance in a world with unlimited choice. Too much choice can make us want to give up before we even start, but it is possible to achieve a good work and life balance, and to have an approach to money that serves us and our communities. Underpinning all this is a strong counterbalance between the emotional and logical parts of our mind.

We will always be dealing with people. Learning how to work well with others – from family members to colleagues and strangers – is one of the most valuable lessons in life. We want our relationships to work. On expeditions – where a breakdown in relations between team members was potentially fatal – I learned the vital importance of effective teamwork.

The adventure of life is ongoing. When one goal is finally reached, we should know what's next. We are always capable of achieving more, and of becoming what we are capable of. No matter what we have – or have not – done up to this point, what matters is how we live the life we have left. Look at the bigger picture. Be open to possibility and opportunity. View life as a journey of adventure and self discovery. Be curious about the world. Have courage.

As the Irish poet John O'Donohue writes, learn "to find ease in risk". Look for the joy in every challenge, no matter how difficult. Dream big. Remember that success lies in the following of the dream. Achieving your goal is a bonus.

We are grateful to Pat Falvey for kind permission to republish this version of one of his pieces.

ABOUT THE AUTHOR

Declan Coyle

Declan is a director of Ireland's most internationally experienced leadership training and development consultants and a much sought after conference keynote speaker. A master practitioner in NLP, he is married with three children. In recent years his motivational and coaching talents has been harnessed by numerous sporting teams. He has multiple international degrees and qualifications, and is fluent in a number of languages, including Mandarin. He is the author of the innovative number one best selling book, 'The Green Platform', an innovative methodology that transforms the morale, productivity and profitability of companies across the globe. His new book, 'Living The Green Platform – Life Changing Stories' contains 90 inspirational columns and is "not about average; it's about fun, it's about hope, and it's about encouragement".

"The purpose of one's life is surely to have a life full of purpose. It's about having a positive impact on as many lives as you possibly can."

DECLAN COYLE

Miracle Walks

DECLAN COYLE

Deep and lasting change is a heroic journey. Sometimes, in our efforts to complete a particular journey in life, we bite off more than we can chew and end up disappointed when we fail. Sometimes, however, we find the hero inside ourselves.

Everything is relative – for some a 5km or 10km walk or run might be that goal, and sometimes people complete shorter, personal journeys that are immense victories for them. I've seen such achievements completed with courage and conviction. Some were over 26 miles long and others only five steps.

Some years ago I had the privilege of introducing Muhammad Ali to an Irish audience in Dublin at a charity dinner organised by Dr Pearse Lyons and the Alltech company. I was backstage with the great man and his wife, Lonnie, as the MC was talking to the audience. Ali was sitting in a chair, shaking with his Parkinson's disease.

My script was simple. Just to say, with as much power and passion as possible, "And now, ladies and gentlemen, a big warm Irish céad míle fáilte for the greatest, Muhammad Ali." And also to give Ali the nod to stand up and walk to the curtain as I bellowed out the boxing ring introduction.

I nodded at Ali to be sure he was okay. He nodded back. When he stood up, he smiled. Chin up. Head back. He was ready. As he started to walk, I began my introduction as if I was in Madison Square Garden introducing a world championship fight. Within a millisecond I saw clearly that I was speaking more quickly than Ali could put one foot past the other.

I just got as far as saying, "and now ladies and gentlemen a big warm Irish céad míle fáilte for..." but Ali had moved only two steps. His jaw was square. He had the steely determination he needed the nights he fought Joe Frazier, George Foreman and Sonny Liston. He had refused to use a wheelchair and was fighting harder than he did against Foreman, or Frazier, or Liston to walk out and greet his Dublin audience.

I was stuck. I had totally overestimated his walking speed. He took the third step and I said, "A living legend." I paused. He took a fourth step. "The most recognised face on the planet..." and then he took a fifth and, just before he opened the curtain, I said, "The greatest, Muhammad Ali."

He got a standing ovation, the longest I've ever seen or heard. By the time it had ended he had been helped to a chair where he was happy to sit down.

Those five steps had taken an awful lot out of him, but he has been fighting for a bigger cause than just a boxing payday in the three decades since he retired. Lonnie had told me that boxing was only ever a vehicle for him to do what he's doing now, raising millions for his charity as he continues to encourage every man, woman and child in the world to be the greatest they can be.

I was humbled to be beside him as he achieved those five steps with immense courage. I saw the "Rumble in the Jungle," and the "Thrilla in Manila" hero. He did it not because he had to but because he wanted to. It gave him purpose and meaning. And he had proved himself far greater than any of us had ever known him to be.

Our third child Alexander has a rare medical condition called Mowat-Wilson syndrome. He was the first baby in Ireland discovered to be suffering from it. As I write this he is ten years old. He will never talk. He can walk a little only if assisted by Annette, his mother, or his brother Fionn or sister Genevieve, or his godmother Mary, or visiting nurse Liz. They all make his life worthwhile. He hasn't eaten for over eight years because his food reaches his system through a tube into his stomach. He's also doubly incontinent.

In my book, 'The Green Platform', Chapter 11 is about the positive impact Alex has on everyone he meets. It's called

"Alexander the Greatest." He is the most magical and magnetic child imaginable. In our house we are all in awe of him. Every morning he takes a special bus to St Catherine's in Newcastle, Co Wicklow, where the staff do amazing work with him and all of his special needs friends.

A few years ago St Catherine's staged a nativity play before Christmas. Alexander was St Joseph. During rehearsals, he was terrific at knocking on the doors of inns that were closed to travellers with a donkey.

However, during the performance, as soon as he saw the audience, he became more interested in waving and clapping his hands on stage than knocking on doors. As some of the actors were in wheelchairs, and others needed assistance to stand up, members of staff were helping them to move around.

In the midst of this, Alexander stood up and walked five steps across the stage on his own unaided. Jane, who looks after his class, was over the moon. Afterwards she was so excited. "Did you see his five steps on his own? Could you even imagine him doing anything like that last year?"

Like Ali, with those five steps in the play, he had proved far greater than any of us ever knew him to be.

So, if you've given up on exercise, working to get promotion, or any other personal challenge, remember Ali and Alex, and realise what you are capable of in your life. Their "marathons" were just five steps each but what a magnificent achievement for both of them. Your journey of 1,000 miles begins with just one step.

Every day is a new beginning for you to start your own heroic journey, inspired by "The Greatest, Muhammad Ali," and "Alexander The Greatest". You too can become the greatest you can be.

Ballpoint Press, publisher of Declan Coyle's The Green Platform series, has granted us kind permission to republish this version of one of Declan's pieces.

ABOUT THE AUTHOR

Emily Gowor

Emily Gowor is an inspirational, multiple award-winning, published author, a professional speaker and mentor, as well as the creator of the revolutionary five-step tool in human potential, the 'Inspiration Formula'. Emily has harnessed her early love of human psychology to build a thriving career bringing writing and inspiration to the world. The author of several published books, Emily's award-winning blog, 'Life Travels in 2010 and 2011', has attracted thousands of online readers. Emily was a winner of the 2012 and 2014 Anthill "30 under 30 Young Entrepreneur Award", and continues her mission to assist people to live deeply meaningful lives. A master certified NLP practitioner and trained facilitator in The Demartini Method®, Emily finds continual inspiration in the divine order of the universe and brings her love for humanity to the forefront into all she does. For more, see www.emilygowor.com

"Choose that you will turn this life into what you dream – no matter what."
EMILY GOWOR

From Depression To Inspiration

EMILY GOWOR

'I don't care if my heart doesn't ever beat again', was the thought running through my mind as, aged 19, I lay on the floor one night in 2007. After discovering that academia wasn't my calling in life, and having dropped out of a university degree in Sociology and Philosophy the year before, I experienced an intense eight-month-long state of what most people would call depression. I didn't care about socialising, I didn't feel like studying, and the idea of being in a relationship felt empty. I had no inclination to do anything that 'normal' people did, including working and earning money.

A friend of mine was paying my bills at the time, and adults in my life were nudging me to get a job, but I was too lost in my own private pain to wrap my head around being employed. Life felt pointless. I barely wanted to get up in the morning. The days were a blur, and even friendships and family began to lose their meaning. It didn't matter what happened, who I saw, or what I did on any day.

On the inside, I was hurting. I felt alone, helpless, misunderstood, believing that neither I nor the life I was living meant anything to the world. I felt insignificant. In that state, it was extremely difficult to see what of any value I had to offer, what destiny I might fulfil on earth, or, as my teachers and mentors believed, that I had greatness within me. I kept searching and questioning but had almost given up on myself. But then, one particular night this all changed.

By the middle of 2007 I had reached the end of my rope. Hopelessness washed over me. I had hit a dead-end, and had no idea what to do or where to turn. While I was driving my car from the south-west suburbs into Brisbane heading north on the freeway, I began to contemplate the idea of ending my life. Driving at about 80km per hour, I eyed the concrete barrier separating the alternating lanes of traffic. "What if I just write myself off, right here, right now?" I thought. "The pain will end. I won't have to do this anymore". I turned the wheel to the right and steered towards the barrier … and then I turned it back. Taking a deep breath, I tried to summon enough courage to actually wipe my presence off the planet, turned the wheel towards the barrier a second time … and turned it back again. I couldn't do it. As well as my human instincts saving me from myself, something from deep within me was saying, "No … this isn't your time. This isn't the way you're going to go."

The human part of me was frustrated, as though I'd let myself down by not being brave enough to relieve myself of pain but, coming so close to the edge of my own existence, had woken something higher in me, my soul, my greater being – whatever you want to call it.

I drove home, parked on the street and walked in the front door of my apartment feeling numb. I dropped my keys onto the kitchen bench and lay down on the mattress that was on the floor of the lounge. For 12 long hours. I didn't move or eat or talk to anyone, and didn't go to the bathroom. I was a bright, smart, and attractive 19-year-old who felt I didn't have anything to live for. In that moment I was incredibly raw, and felt I had been stripped bare – it was as if I was drowning – and a part of me that knew that life didn't have to be this way, that we aren't put here on earth to suffer.

Deep down inside, I knew that human beings aren't born without purpose or the ability to thrive in the pursuit and expression of it. Perhaps I wasn't as insignificant as I thought I was, and convincing myself that neither my life nor I mattered was a lie I'd been telling myself. In that moment, I made a life-altering, destiny-forming decision, that I would do whatever it took to live an extraordinary life. The decision was based on two things – that taking my life was not an option anymore, and that I yearned to experience something magnificent, inspiring, and deeply meaningful. I didn't really want my life to end, quite the opposite. I wanted to live fully, longed to express what I knew was inside me, and wanted to spend my life fulfilling my mission as a writer, painting a picture of the world more beautiful than anything people could ordinarily have imagined.

It was all on me to make sure that manifested itself, and the effort to keep this up for the rest of my life would remain with me. I didn't care: I wanted in. In that moment, lying on the floor, and feeling more alone, depressed and down-and-out than ever before, I made the decision to be in. I let go of who I thought I should be, and accepted myself for who I was. Finally I let the past be the past. And I found the determination and drive that I needed to make my dreams come true, for my own sake, and the sake of others feeling beaten down by life. From that moment, I became incredibly committed to the pursuit and fulfilment of what mattered most: a commitment that is every bit as forceful today.

The journey to transform my life didn't happen overnight, but it did happen. I began working hard on myself. I did over three hours of personal development every day for about eight months, the same length of time I had been feeling depressed. I examined every feeling, every thought, and every part of my mind and heart, leaving no stone unturned. I used the work of Dr John Demartini and my Master Certification in NLP (Neuro-Linguistic Programming) to self-heal. Gradually, through attending to myself, my life began to feel less like an abyss of meaninglessness. The true, radiant me began to emerge from underneath the wounds of the past.

A matter of months later I rediscovered my love of writing and, by way of synchronicity, soon after, a contact asked a question that altered my life: "Did you know you can be paid to write?" At the time I was working in retail, selling books, having rediscovered my drive, desire and 'why' to work again. My ears pricked up. I jumped at the opportunity he presented to write an article about him which would be published in an entrepreneurs' magazine in 2008. There began my journey to be who I am and where I am today. Quickly I grew my profile as a paid professional writer. The pursuit of what I not only loved but lived to do, led me to truly great places. In 2009 I was blessed to edit the first manuscript of Dr John Demartini's best-selling book for Hay House, Inspired Destiny. That same year, I was offered the chance to write my first book with a publishing company in New Zealand. My dream of being an author came true when I was just 23 years old.

Fast-forward ten years from my own moment of destiny, and it's hard to reflect on this, my life hasn't followed my wish when lying on the floor of my apartment that my heart wouldn't ever beat again. Realising that my heart beating is actually the most important thing of all is what has driven me – all before the age of 30 – to write eight books, speak internationally, blog my way around the world, be interviewed in media, establish a publishing company, be paid richly to do what I love, win multiple young entrepreneur awards, and unite communities in global projects. My memories of that moment where I nearly ended it all are what enable me to inspire other people as I draw on my own story for inspiration in the moments I need it most.

Today, I am certain that the people who believed in and gave a determined young woman the chance to serve and grow are the ones I have to thank for much of what I have achieved in the first ten years of my adult life. However, had I not taken the time to be alone and feel what I felt at 19, when the sky seemed to be falling in, I wouldn't be here. Had I not experienced my rock-bottom, literally a do-or-die moment, I wouldn't have found the mission that drives me today. My mission is to bring books and inspiration to the world.

The moral of my story is not only that it is possible to transform your life from being down-and-out, to being alive, gloriously purposeful, doing what you love, and touching the world – but also the certainty that, when you step forward, life meets you halfway. When you make the choice not only to live, but to live fully, life shows up. When you want to fly, life helps you to find your wings and puts air beneath them.

The key to everything is to choose. Decide that you are not done with your life, and that, like me, you are going to do whatever it takes to make it an extraordinary one. I believe to my heart's core that this is not only what you deserve, but what you were born for. So choose ... to find your inspiration and pursue it down every path that beckons ... choose to overcome your past and let your bright future call to you. And choose that you will turn this life into what you dream – no matter what.

ABOUT THE AUTHOR

Jillian Godsil

Jillian Godsil is a writer working and living in south Wicklow. Deeply affected by the global economic tsunami of 2009, she lost her husband to divorce, her home to the banks, and her dignity to the world. She kept her two beautiful daughters, whom she loves with a passion. When speaking of her children she often tears up – much to their annoyance. Right now she is writing the most beautiful book in the world. Her motto is 'Onwards and upwards, maybe sideways but never backwards' (actually her mother's). For more, see www.jilliangodsil.com.

"Onwards and upwards, maybe sideways,
but never backwards"
JILLIAN GODSIL

A Political Life

JILLIAN GODSIL

Extracts from my blog *Running the Race*:
Sunday morning 25 May 2014

I have run the race and am reaching the end. I have yet to cross
the line but it is in sight. My legs are sore, my breathing laboured,
and there are rubs on my feet. There are many ahead of me; a
goodly pack of politicians, first timers, old timers, new seekers,
tired thinkers, young ones, old ones and in-between ones. There
are even one or two stragglers behind me. We have all run our
race, some with parties, some without, some with zeal, some
with polish, some with ideas quite divergent, and some with
ideas that are as old as the earth.

In this race there were moments when people slipped, were
pushed or just fell. Mostly the other runners skipped over or
ran around the runner on the ground. It was rare a hand was
held out by another runner; it is not that kind of race. But it was

common for the spectators to rush forward and pull the runner to his feet, to push water into his hand and to chivvy him on his way.

When I first put my name forward for this race, my friend and neighbour Tony said to me: "Are you cotton pickin mad?" And I looked him in the eye and said, "Yes." But I had it worked out in my head. It was never about getting elected; it was always about making a difference.

This was the same conversation I had with Deputy Shane Ross; one of the first people I spoke with about running, and who subsequently gave me the highest compliment possible; giving me his endorsement along with campaigner Diarmuid O'Flynn with a ringing cry, "two noble independent battlers – both deserve seats."

The prize I wanted was the race itself. I wanted to use my time to talk about the burning issue at the heart of my personal campaign for the past three years, the unjust treatment of Irish families in debt. I wanted to stop the vilification of people in debt. I wanted to change the law and language, and the bullying.

Of course, there were times along the way when the voice of pride spoke into my ear. You can win, it said softly and sinuously. You can take a seat. You can go to Europe. I listened but shook my head. Winning was never about getting elected, whatever selfish pride might say. I knew from the start that my message, while loudspeaker noisy, was unlikely to translate into medals.

Still, when I heard my vote from the local count last night I was saddened a little. Each vote I got was humbling, each vote I didn't get was equally so.

So, as I prepare to travel down to Cork to meet my fellow European candidates, I do so with the right kind of pride in my heart, the pride of having run the race to the end, of having treated my fellow candidates with respect. The pride of helping where I could, and certainly not harming where I was able. The pride of having stood shoulder to shoulder as we prepared for war; under the lights of the TV cameras, before the microphones in the studio, or caught in the glare of the inquisitor searching for the truth.

To my fellow combatants: I salute you on the race run. I am honoured to have run beside you, behind you and sometimes (in a rare moment) even in front of some of you.

And as I come to end of the race I ran, my wish is that people remember what I stood for and what I will continue to stand for until such time as fairness, justice and truth are the norm. And now the fat lady sings. For the hidden pain of debt – I think in hymns. And I thank you for allowing me to run the race.

And I cross the line...

Have you ever thought of becoming a politician? Not just shouting at the telly when the news is on, or sharing damning articles on Facebook, or ranting and raving on a bar stool, but the real McCoy, an actual politician? A real live, walking, talking politician. No? Yet, in 2014 that was what happened to me. I shook off the uniform of civilian and took on the mantle of political candidate. How on earth did that happen to a nice, middle aged woman like me?

Like the Irish novelist Laurence Sterne, I'd love to go back to the very beginning, but then we might never actually reach 2014, at least not within the confines of this article. And brevity, as we are told, is the soul of wit.

So how did I arrive in Cork in April 2014 to hand over assentor forms that allowed me to put my name forward for the 2014 European Parliamentary Election? I had to strong-arm 60 good and true burghers to say they knew me, and get a guard to witness their statements, as I did not have enough money for a deposit. But why was I standing there before the returning officer in Cork clutching this passport to the elections? In the preceding ten years I had ended my marriage, lost my home, my business had collapsed, and then I had become bankrupt. It was a very tough ten years – a slow slide into poverty and near destitution with my two children by my side. I had become an accidental politician.

Along the way I had discovered a powerful truth, that, in Ireland, financial failure is considered shameful. In the middle of the biggest global recession in almost 100 years Irish people were failing financially and blaming themselves. And, if they had managed to retain their dignity, then there were plenty of people willing to kick them in the teeth. One woman told me, "I was brought up to repay my debts." That was a sucker punch. Obviously she thought I hadn't been.

As I slipped down the rabbit hole of poverty, I kept shouting that I was not ashamed. And I kept slipping inexorably. Yes, there was pain, but no shame.

Finally, when I became the first female bankrupt under the new Irish insolvency laws, I discovered that I was not allowed to run for public office. So I dug my heels in and said enough, no more. I challenged the Irish Government in the High Court, and eventually in the Supreme Court, claiming that my constitutional rights were being infringed. I was not a criminal, and being bankrupt should not disqualify me from running for public office. My case was successful, and so I ran for Europe.

I toured the country, knocked on doors and spoke on endless radio programmes and TV channels. I had six glorious weeks. In the final week I made some fabulous clangers. On 'Prime Time' I told Claire Byrne that I knew nothing about Europe and that I was going there to find out and tell Ireland all about it. On 'Vincent Browne' my opening line was that I was Protestant, divorced and on the pill. At the time it made sense, and it caused untold merriment, as well as a few shaking heads, up and down the country. And then the polls closed.

The result? I topped the Independent tally from Wicklow and exited the European race on 11,500 votes. Not bad for an independent, nil budget candidate with a month to canvas in total. However, I did badly in the local elections.

It was a bewildering place to be. Running for office is a bruising process. Political candidates put themselves out to be judged. I was humbled that I had received a low count in Wicklow, and confused that I had received the top tally for Ireland South in the same county. I wrote my blog that morning. The most important line in it was that every vote that came my way humbled me, as did every vote I didn't get.

I posted my blog and headed to the count centre in Cork intending to stay only a few hours. Three days later, they had to peel me out of the place. I sloughed off my half-formed political career and drove home in a kind of delirium. For six weeks I had been hounded by every person, club, advocacy group and organisation going. My opinion had been sought on every topic under the sun. I was on a huge learning curve to figure out my thoughts on all these diverse topics, realising that it might matter. And, afterwards, came silence.

Being a political candidate is like having a birthday on Facebook. For a brief intense period of time everyone wants a piece of you, sends you a message, pictures, gifs and videos. Then it goes very quiet. You are no longer the birthday girl. You are no longer the political candidate. It is over. And then you give thanks.

ABOUT THE AUTHOR

Dermot Higgins

Addicted to the outdoor life from an early age, Dermot Higgins became interested in endurance sports when he began primary-level teaching 35 years ago. He ran, and participated in triathlons and mountain running. Since discovering kayaking, Dermot has organised numerous kayaking expeditions on many of Ireland's rivers, lakes and canals. He has toured the island of Ireland on his bicycle. Dermot is retiring from teaching and planning an epic circumnavigation of the world by bicycle, aiming to become the oldest person ever to have completed this feat. Dermot's favourite quote is Aristotle's "Adventure is worthwhile".

"Full wise is he that can himself know."
GEOFFREY CHAUCER (THE CANTERBURY TALES)

Easter Pilgrims

DERMOT HIGGINS

This would be our most ambitious kayaking expedition to date. Fionn, who hadn't yet turned ten, and I would paddle across Ireland north to south and east to west. We estimated the total distance to be just shy of 400km, or 240 miles. Our plan was to travel for seven days at an average daily speed of 3.5mph for 35 miles. In order to achieve this, we would be paddling for ten hours every day. We would set out on the Irish Sea from the docks in Dublin and, via the canal and river network, reach Ballyshannon on the Atlantic Ocean a week later on Easter Sunday.

Our 20ft long vessel of choice was the Chrisobel 111. She's made of fibreglass and has two keyhole cockpits. Nearly as old as myself, she's a veteran of many voyages on high seas and rivers. She's been holed and repaired so many times over the years that it's impossible to prevent water from seeping in. However, she's light and sleek, and capable of making four to five knots in good conditions on flat water.

As on previous trips, we decided to be as self-sufficient as possible. We brought considerable quantities of cereals, rice, dried milk powder, some fresh vegetables, and 2kg of cheese. The food was stored in a watertight barrel secured to the kayak by bungees. We included a small single ring gas burner, a cook-set with dishes and cutlery, fishing lines, nets, head-torches, sunscreen, mobile phone for emergencies, and an indispensable hand-pump. We planned to camp along the banks and to source food en route by foraging, fishing and hunting.

We also carried our lightweight Vango expedition tent, self-inflating sleep mats, pillows (that doubled as back-rests) and winter sleeping bags. We each carried a spare paddling kit, and two sets of warm, dry civilian clothes. Sleeping bags, pillows and clothing were stuffed into two big dry bags to be stowed at our feet in the kayak. We also planned to lash a fold-up bicycle to the deck of the kayak to allow Fionn to cycle along the canal tow paths when he tired of paddling.

So, after rushed preparations – the previous night I'd celebrated my 50th birthday – we were at last ready to launch our fully loaded kayak from Spencer Dock in Dublin's docklands at 2pm on Sunday 1 April.

We certainly felt like proper April fools ten minutes later. A large crowd – mostly curious kids expecting some fun had gathered to witness the launch. Slowly we lowered the kayak over the jetty into the water. But the weight of the bicycle and food barrel shifted suddenly as she hit the water causing her to keel over, capsize and sink slowly into the dock. I'd no option other than to jump in after her to try to halt her descent into the murky depths. Much to the amusement of the assembled kids, I had to swim after the food barrel and assorted items of clothing, and dive down to retrieve the bicycle. Fionn proved his worth by tracking down helpful passers-by who assisted with the subsequent bailing and pump-out. Eventually we were left with a sodden mess of gear and clothing on the jetty. At the end of that day's expedition, we hadn't covered even a single metre of the 400 we'd planned. Our support team (my wife and daughter), kindly returned to collect us and so we returned home, tails between our legs, to rethink, and reload.

The following day saw a trimmed down operation, the bicycle abandoned, and the weight of provisions and clothing greatly reduced. We experimented with different options for lashing and loading and, at last, were satisfied that we could get going.

Our second launch was as smooth as could be. As the kayak glided effortlessly through the still waters of the Royal Canal in Dublin's western suburbs and out into the broad expanses of the Counties Kildare and Meath countryside, we were in high spirits. We reached Maynooth for lunch, and powered on to Moyvalley as dusk was falling. We set up camp a metre from the water beside Furey's pub. The barman welcomed us warmly into the bar where we had a blast chatting and filming the locals, and eventually, well fed and watered, we snuggled down to sleep in our warm, waterside tent.

For the next six days we followed a broadly similar pattern. I'd wake at 7.30am, answer the inevitable call of nature, have a quick wash in the river, prepare muesli for me, and Coco Pops for Fionn, using up whatever scraps we had left over from the previous night's dinner. After two mugs of good coffee I'd wake Fionn. We'd finish breakfast, wash up, strike camp, reload all the gear and food, struggle into cold and wet paddling clothes and prepare to launch. Most days we were on the water by ten o'clock.

We didn't take a morning break and paddled non-stop right up to 2pm or so, when we'd haul up at a sheltered spot by a bridge or lock for half an hour's lunch break. We snacked on thick slices of cheese, chocolate and swallowed a warm brew. We'd resume paddling without delay and power on till dusk, normally about 8pm. Once we were forced to paddle on into the dark in order to reach our pre-planned camping point.

Many people are amazed that it's possible to undertake ten hours or more of almost continuous paddling every day for a whole week, but it actually becomes easier and more enjoyable as time goes on. The rhythmic nature of the paddling induces an almost trance-like experience. Conversation ebbs and flow. The scenery along the riverbank is ever-changing and always enthralling.

Of course, there were times when we struggled against strong headwinds, or blisters on our palms made paddling painful, but, sooner or later, we'd reach a point when it all became almost effortless. We stroked rhythmically together, father and son united, bodies and souls united, untiring muscles bulging, like a well oiled machine powering through wind and wave. It's a truly awesome feeling when this state kicks in and maintains the perpetual forward motion for ages. On the river time has no meaning. Hours slip by in the blink of an eyelid, and finally you're again safe and dry in your campsite, tranquil waters gurgling quietly in the background.

The weather gods weren't at all kind to us on our long pilgrimage to the West. During that week temperatures struggled to reach double digits by day, and in the midlands, night-time temperatures plummeted to -5° on two consecutive nights. In the mornings we had to wait for our paddling gear to thaw and soften before we could get into it! Far worse than the cold was the wind that came from the north and west directly into our faces, bringing rain, hail, sleet and on one occasion, even snow.

The other serious difficulty we encountered came in dealing with the canal locks that enable the man-made canals to climb and drop down over the slight midland gradients. There are 46 locks on the Royal Canal and 16 on the Shannon/Erne Waterway. Due to low water levels, we weren't allowed to manually open and close the lock gates on the Royal. We were forced to drag our kayak, and 50kg of gear, over each and every one of them.

People ask what were the high and low points. My highlight happened late one evening as we were approaching Jamestown on the Shannon. Darkness had descended, and a light drizzle was falling. Fionn had nodded off asleep in front of me, and I was at the edge of exhaustion. Suddenly, on silent wings, a barn owl swooped alongside us. As it disappeared into the gloom I caught a brief glimpse of its eyes. It was a moment of pure magic.

Fionn claims that the high point for him was waking up surprised to find himself in a dry, cozy bed on Sunday morning. We had expected to camp at the Share Holiday Village at Smith's Strand near Lisnaskea in Co Fermanagh on Saturday night, but the kind-hearted staff took pity on us and offered us a room for the night in their quarters.

Although we can laugh about it now, the lowest point for each of us was the calamity at Spencer Dock on April Fool's Day. Though it seemed like a disaster, we learned never to overload a boat again. Fionn hated it when a rare navigational error took us an hour off course up the very stinky River Camlin in Longford. The smell of slurry was a constant companion throughout the midlands. He was also disgusted by the levels of pollution we witnessed. It was often agricultural waste, but near the towns and villages there was a mix of plastic packaging and tin cans. And, once, we almost speared a dead sheep floating in the canal in Leitrim.

What we encountered in abundance along the banks was prolific wildlife. We saw all three types of swan – Whooper, Mute and Bewick – various species of ducks and waders, kingfishers flashing like jewels in the gloom, and the first of the summer swallows flying low over the Fermanagh lakelands. We saw otters, minks and foxes. The sheer exuberance of springtime bursting from the hedgerows was a joy to witness.

We reached our destination, palms blistered, bums chafed and nearly 6kg lighter than at the start. But we got there in the end, safe and sound.

People ask why did we consider this to have been a pilgrimage as well as an expedition. We felt proud and strangely humbled by the experience. We were elated as well as exhausted by the journey. It had added a new dimension to my being, to my relationship with my family and with the earth. Like Chaucer's pilgrims in the 14th century Canterbury Tales, our travels had taught us much about ourselves.

ABOUT THE AUTHOR

Samantha Kelly

A leading social media strategist, speaker and trainer, Samantha owns and operates "Tweeting Goddess". With her team, Samantha plans and delivers effective social media strategies to businesses and entrepreneurs, harnessing the power of social media and the online community. She has delivered training courses to many businesses including Hewlett Packard, HSE and the Irish League of Credit Unions. Samantha is founder of Social Media Summit Ireland and co-founder of the Women's Inspire Network. She is the proud mum of two beautiful girls and lives in Rosslare Harbour, Co Wexford, Ireland.

"I'm no longer that girl with no confidence who fears she has nothing to offer. I now feel like a useful member of society."
SAMANTHA KELLY

From Social Welfare To Social Media Influencer

SAMANTHA KELLY

When I was younger, even though I was always a hard worker, I drifted in and out of jobs, not quite settling anywhere. I did temping work as a receptionist, and had lots of sales and customer service roles. When I was a waitress, I always made great tips as I knew how to talk to people and offered excellent customer service. I always went above and beyond what was expected of me, and loved dealing with people, but I wasn't so great at taking orders from a boss. And, somehow, I was never that happy staying in one place for long. I was adaptable, and a fast learner, but doing what I was asked to do was never my strong point. I was feisty, stubborn at times, and not a good listener. I was also very sensitive, and, being honest, still can be.

When I had my first daughter, I wasn't in a good relationship, so I left and went off on my own. I'd lost a lot of confidence, and didn't think I had anything to offer, so I relied on social welfare. I didn't quite know what I wanted to do. And, as with lots of lone parents, I didn't have childcare in place and couldn't get out to find a proper job. Eventually I divorced, remarried, and had my second daughter, but again I was unfulfilled, and wanted to do something, but didn't know what. What was my purpose? I was a bit lost. I felt a failure and also felt very lonely. By this stage I had started relying a bit more on alcohol.

In 2011 my father passed away, and that really pushed me into action. I felt, 'You only live once' and decided it was time to do something, but still didn't know what that something was. I changed my whole way of thinking and, slowly but surely, started to realise that, in fact, I had some talents and something to offer. Almost nine years later, I don't drink.

My second marriage had broken down, and my second daughter, who is hearing-impaired with severe language delay, was about to start mainstream school. I was on a carer's allowance at this stage, and I was hitting the big 40. All my ducks were lined up in a row...

One day, when my older daughter came to that awkward milestone of puberty, I went searching for a gift to make her transition to womanhood easier. I couldn't find a starter set for girls, so I came up with the idea for 'Funky Goddess'. I had absolutely no money at all, and didn't have a great record with the banks, so I went on 'Dragons' Den' on TV. This was when, in the public mind, my journey really started.

Before I went on the show, I started to use social media, in particular Twitter, to market Funky Goddess, and discovered that I was pretty hot at it. I was actually talking to people, dealing with them, and 'building relationships', even though I didn't realise it. When the girls were in bed, I was talking to people on Twitter. I gleaned as much as I could online about Twitter, and social media in general.

By the time I went on 'Dragons' Den', I had already gained a following of over 5,000 people. So, even though a money investment from the show didn't materialise, I kept going after 'Dragons' Den'. I was determined to succeed. However, I needed to make a profit, so, in the end, I had to shelve Funky Goddess, and earn money. I couldn't keep going as I was, especially as, one day, my daughters and I were sitting by the fire, but had no coal. I decided that I couldn't keep doing this to my children.

What happened next was really interesting. A local hotel, struggling with their Twitter account, approached me and asked could I help them with it. This was my first client.

Again, I got that moment where I thought, 'hang on, perhaps I have a business here'. All I did was talk to the followers they already had, and build relationships with new customers, and the hotel's clicks to sale went up fifteen percent. I decided to rebrand, and sold Funky Goddess to a customer. And this was really how it all kicked off for 'Tweeting Goddess'.

So now that I was Tweeting Goddess, people slagged me about the name. "Who does she think she is?", "She could do with losing a few pounds, she is over 40 for goodness sake!" etc etc … but I noticed, in the USA in particular, that they loved the name Tweeting Goddess. I mean, it does what it says on the tin!

I have built some awesome relationships on Twitter, and have spoken to and met people from all over the world. Conversations I start on Twitter with people I admire have led to a Skype call or coffee. Also, people are watching all the time, so I've had folk say they love my tweets, and I'm like, how cool that that person actually knows who I am!'

I always tweet tips and write articles that show I know my stuff. And I am constantly helping others, especially start-ups and small business owners, as I've been there and know what it's like having no marketing budget!

I wanted to learn more and more. I wanted to be the top Twitter expert, and also to learn as much as I could from experts in other platforms. Now I have over 37,000 followers. I have created communities online on Twitter and Facebook, such as Womensinspirenetwork.com. It was so difficult to find an event that covered all of the social media platforms, and an event where I could learn how to be better, and get results for clients, so I created my own, the Social Media Summit, now in its second year, thanks to Cogs and Marvel. In 2017 we had Mari Smith, one of the world's leading social media thought leaders, and Forbes' #4 "Top Social Media Power Influencer" at the summit in Dublin. I was now one of the top influencers in Ireland on Social Media and was featured on many lists, such as 'Top 21 All-Star Twitter Marketers to follow', and many others. I also had a verified Twitter account.

At events I started sharing my knowledge with others. The more I showed I was an expert in what I did, the more requests came in to speak at other events. I love to meet others who were in my situation, and it's a lovely feeling to be able to inspire others. I even got asked to do a TED talk.

Thanks to Twitter my whole life has changed. I'm no longer that girl with no confidence who fears she has nothing to offer. I now feel like a useful member of society, knowing that I give real value to other people, although I never forget where I came from.

This is my big 'Thank You' to all of the fab people I've met along the way. The next stop, I hope, will be speaking in the USA. Dreams do come true, so I have that on my vision board!

Link to Samantha Kelly's TED talk: https://www.youtube.com/watch?v=K40PGZy6oe8

ABOUT THE AUTHOR

Breifne Earley

Happiest when lost in nature, hiking mountain tops, or on two wheels, adventurer, speaker and author Breifne Earley is looking to inspire others to live a positive life. His achievements include winning the longest endurance sporting event in the world, writing a bestselling book, creating the "Cloud9 Conference", and coaching numerous football teams to national and European successes. He is frightened of rollercoasters, loves being active, playing music, binge watching TV shows, and going to the cinema alone during the day. Breifne shares his inspiring story in workplaces and schools around the globe. For more, see www.breifneearley.com.

"We could be heroes, just for one day."
DAVID BOWIE (HEROES)

True Heroes

BREIFNE EARLEY

Whenever I hear the word 'hero' I can't but hear the distinctive opening strains to David Bowie's hit, a song that I first became aware of during the hosting of the Special Olympics in Ireland back in 2003. It's one of a number of terms that get used regularly in our day-to-day lives to describe, in some cases, quite everyday events. 'Legend', 'Epic', 'Celebrity', 'Saint' and 'God' would be some others that don't sit well with me when used to describe some people's status, deeds or accomplishments.

Each of these words have been used to describe me and my own achievements at some point, whether it's about my cycle around the world, writing and publishing a best-selling book, or just turning my life around from a very low point, when I was facing the prospect of suicide, to where such undertakings became normal to me.

The reality is that I'm not a hero, I'm just a guy who decided to take control of his life, and then found myself on a bicycle cycling 30,000km around the entire planet. My book 'Pedal The Planet' was the final leg of that journey. I wasn't the one to turn it into a bestseller, the people who bought it and supported me along the way made that happen.

For me a hero is someone who, every day, goes above and beyond what is best for everyone, and not just themselves, someone who puts the needs and wants of those deemed lesser, on a par with their own. Through work and friends, I've been lucky enough to meet a lot of high profile people over the years, and I'm going to share with you personal encounters with three of my heroes, and why I deem them worthy of the title.

My earliest sporting memories would have been of watching Ireland progress through Italia '90 to the quarter finals against Italy where Toto Schillaci would eventually end our dreams. The penalty shoot-out against Romania burned an image in my brain forever, particularly Packie Bonner's save. Diving low to his right, he saved Romania's final spot kick, setting it up for David O'Leary to win the game.

The following summer, finding myself in goal for Carrick Town's under 12s in a penalty shoot-out, we were in a similar position with a single kick each. I dived the same way as Packie Bonner, got a hand to the ball and kept it out, with my team mate stepping up to send us into the cup final. It was our own world cup victory.

Fifteen years later, I was working full time in Sport HQ, where the FAI's technical department would hold monthly staff meetings.

As Technical Director, Bonner was in charge of the department and the 50 or so staff working there.

Every month the FAI guys would breeze into our small shared canteen, catered food and drinks laid out neatly, organised especially for the blow ins. With no canteen staff, normally each person was responsible for their own rubbish and for cleaning up after themselves. After 20 minutes the FAI guys would just up and depart, leaving behind half full glasses, remnants of meals on paper plates, and general chaos.

As the man in charge, Packie would have been forgiven for being the first out the door, but he always stayed behind, cleaned up after his staff, returned furniture to original positions, until there wasn't a sign that they had even been there.

Katie Taylor has long been the darling of Irish sport. Since she burst onto the scene in 2012 winning a boxing Gold Medal at the London Olympics we just can't get enough of her achievements, successes and setbacks. Katie's 'overnight success' wasn't a surprise to anyone involved in Irish sport over the last ten or 15 years.

As a novice women's football coach in the early noughties, I knew all about Katie, an international player who'd been setting the world alight in the underage ranks. At the time, there was a rumour that she also did a bit of boxing.

When I was asked to take over a struggling UCD side in the 2005/06 college football season, I inherited a team that included

Taylor. She was already a European and World Champion in boxing, and a senior international in soccer. She was a model professional in terms of her preparation and commitment to both sports.

The following season, now looking after the regional Leinster Universities team, I invited Katie to be part of the squad for the upcoming Inter Provincials' competition. Well aware of her pedigree and availability, I explained that she didn't need to participate in the trial game that we had organised a few weeks later. She insisted that she would play, although asking to be excused for the second half. She didn't feel it would be fair to the other girls if she didn't participate in the trials.

On the day of the game, she played out of her skin. As agreed, she left at the interval. When I got home a couple of hours later, I turned on my television. A very differently attired Katie was picking up a 'Sportswoman of the Year' award live on RTE television.

In 2012, a month after Taylor's London exploits, I found myself in the Olympic Stadium watching another Irish hero perform on the world stage. Darragh McDonald and Jason Smyth had already secured their gold medals at the Paralympics, when Michael McKillop took to the track to defend his 2008 Gold medal in the 800 metres. Not only did McKillop win comfortably, he smashed the world record.

Three years earlier I'd had the pleasure of meeting Michael at my alma mater, Dublin City University, during a recruitment day for

Paralympic athletes. The day was designed to allow children with disabilities, and people who were eligible for the Paralympics, to sample what each sport offered. From boccia to rowing, powerlifting to wheelchair rugby, and anything in between, prospective athletes were given the opportunity to experience and even participate in sport, most for the very first time.

One of my favourite memories is of watching twins, one a wheelchair user, playing basketball. Both were put in a basketball chair. They played on opposite teams, as equals, against each other for the first time ever. The delight in the two boys' faces was matched by the tears flowing from their watching mother's eyes.

As a medalist in Beijing, Michael McKillop was one of the star attractions, but after the dust had settled, and the day had drawn to a close, I was helping to tidy up after the event. Michael and myself just started an impromptu kick around with one of the footballs lying about. For 20 minutes we just laughed and joked as we tried to outdo each other with keepie-uppies, just like kids.

His disability, a form of cerebral palsy, never even came up. It never was a factor, as he had long before decided it wasn't a crutch or something to hold him back. It was part of his life, and he would continue to win medals and set world records regardless. He had been the star attraction at this national recruitment event, but he was happiest just having a kick around like most 19 year olds.

These inspiring people's actions taught me that a real hero isn't defined by what happens under the lights, before tens of thousands of eyes in a sports venue, or millions of people on TV, but what they do in their everyday lives.

It's about how they treat others, when they could get away with walking away from a mess, when they are offered a free pass on being selected for a team, or how they interact with a stranger when they have top billing but the crowd has left and the doors are closed.

Sporting achievements come and go. Someone else will win that next race, or take home that medal, or save that penalty, but it's the way we treat those around us, regardless of status, that shows the qualities that define a 'hero'.

ABOUT THE AUTHOR

TeeJay Dowe

TeeJay Dowe is an experienced, energetic and enthusiastic motivational speaker, international coach, master neurostrategist and NLP trainer. She is the author of 'PerfectShun – Permission to be Human'. A journey from pharmacist to neurostrategist and NLP trainer has been an amazing adventure over the last decade and testimony to the fact that you can not only dream bigger dreams but they can come true! With a mission to "inspire you to find the best within yourself in order to give the best of yourself", TeeJay seeks to empower people to find their passion and reach their full potential. Her passion and purpose is to make a difference to the lives of young people, boost their confidence, increase their self-worth, and give them a sense of vision, direction and purpose. She works with young people everywhere, and trains youth coaches in advanced youth coaching skills.

"Nothing bad ever happens to us, just things that feel bad. It is only later that we see it brought about a shift in our thinking or circumstances and created an opportunity in the future."
TEEJAY DOWE

Negative Emotions Are a Gift

TEEJAY DOWE

It might be hard to believe but so called 'negative emotions' have a value. Think about it. They were designed to be painful or uncomfortable or unpleasant to make sure that you get the message quickly and move on! We feel them for a reason. They are an integral, built-in guidance system, a human emotional SatNav! We can use them.

Back in the days when I worked at the local hospital as a pharmacy technician, I was discovering who I was. I compensated for painful shyness by being especially outgoing with trusted friends, and I expressed myself with the clothes I wore and my hair styles. I was a bit of a rebel.

In my work I was conscientious and held myself to the highest standards, and I wanted to prove that people shouldn't be judged by appearance but by their professionalism and attention to detail. I worked with fabulous people and I got along with everyone in the department, with everyone except the boss. I don't mean my immediate boss – that relationship was fine – but the overall boss of the local hospitals' pharmacy service. She took a dislike to me within my first few weeks when she spotted me wearing a pair of quite trendy and fashionable, but not outrageous, boots in the courtyard. They were different to what others might wear for work.

I was new and didn't actually realise who she was. She made a comment I didn't understand, and it went downhill from then on. The comments about my appearance continued during her visits to the department, and later turned to threats. I qualified as a technician and was warned, in writing, that I could have a job only if I did not wear striped dungarees under my lab coat.

When I wanted to study for a Higher National Diploma, she put obstacles in my way. At first I was not allowed to start as no senior technician positions were available in the department. Then I was turned down because of a lack of funding, so I offered to pay for myself. Then I was stopped because they couldn't afford day cover for me in the department. I offered to take a day less pay and pay for myself. Only when I pointed out that other technicians had done the course, hadn't paid for themselves, did not take less pay, or didn't struggle to have another team member cover their day, and the word 'discrimination' was mentioned, was I finally given the go ahead.

In private, my nemesis made it absolutely clear that she would never allow me to be promoted to a Senior Technician position in that hospital. When she asked why I didn't look for a job somewhere else, that stung. Casually I replied, "Actually I quite like working here. I think I'll stay."

I shrugged it off for a long time, gritted my teeth and carried on. I'd put on a brave front at work, cry at home and look for other jobs, but none were as interesting as the one I had. As promised, I was passed over for several senior positions that I was amply qualified for and had the most appropriate experience in. As the conflict escalated I felt bullied and became angry. Anger turned to determination, and I dug my heels in get some justice.

It got so bad that I involved the unions in a case for unfair treatment and discrimination. It was horrible, and I hated having to do it. Nevertheless, someone needed to make a stand or others would be treated like this. Attending meetings and hearings and collecting evidence etc. took a while but, finally, it was over, and I won! I got the promotion I had waited so long for.

I set up and ran a unit that was new to our pharmacy department, I was senior technician for cytotoxic reconstitution, I prepared cancer drugs for patients on the wards and visited the outpatient clinics. Due to the nature of the work, I worked mostly in isolation, and I loved the responsibility.

One day I remember thinking how blessed I was to have this job. Then, out of nowhere, a thought popped into my head. "Yes," it said, "but what if you don't like it so much in five years' time?

Then what will you do?" What would I do? I could return to the dispensaries, or go into pharmacy stores, pushing a trolley around a windy warehouse picking items off the shelves… And that did not appeal! I could go no further unless I had a degree.

Having fought long and hard to get where I was, I had never looked beyond that. But that old battle was won. It was time to use the determination that got me to this place to reach towards the next level. In order to keep moving forward, we need more and more goals, and I wanted a "what next" objective. I used my precious HNC to apply to university to do a pharmacy degree and, against the odds, got accepted. And I have never looked back!

A series of negative events led to life changing opportunities simply because I used my emotional resources. Had I got on well with that boss all those years ago, I would probably still be working away as a pharmacy technician instead of making a difference in the world and impacting the lives and wellbeing of hundreds of people. Without all that, I doubt I would feel so passionately about ensuring that young people know that they do not need to settle for second best, that they don't have to give in to bullies.

I totally believe that nothing bad ever happens to us, just things that feel bad. At the time we can't look back and don't understand why something needed to happen. It is only later that we see it brought about a shift in our thinking or circumstances and created an opportunity in the future. That belief got me through challenging situations in my own life, and will continue to serve me.

ABOUT THE AUTHOR

Roger James Hamilton

Roger Hamilton, a futurist and social entrepreneur living in Bali, believes that the entrepreneur movement will solve our greatest global challenges. He is the founder of Entrepreneurs Institute, a community of 1,000,000+ entrepreneurs, mentors and investors in 90 countries. In his late 20s, Roger moved from London to Singapore to establish Free Market Media, and launched 28 local community newspapers in property, living and travel. He devised 'Wealth Dynamics', a profiling system which is used by some 400,000 entrepreneurs around the world, and the Genius Test, Passion Test and Purpose Test. He is also the founder of GeniusU, a fast growth tech startup, and the author of several books including the best selling 'The Millionaire Master Plan' in 2016.

"Everyone is a genius, but if we judge a fish on its ability to climb a tree, it will spend its whole life believing it's stupid."

ALBERT EINSTEIN

Follow Your Genius

ROGER JAMES HAMILTON

In Hong Kong, Christmas 1988, I was 19 years old, sitting and talking with my parents, brother and sister about where I wanted to be in 30 years. We all fantasised about owning a resort on a paradise island where we could spend time together and live in nature. We weren't wealthy, and had no way to afford a resort, but my childhood spent on the beaches of Papua New Guinea had been happy. There was no way that Hong Kong could compete with that.

That Christmas Day, we all agreed that my dream was a wonderful dream, but that was all it was, and I went off to college to be an architect. In my fifth year of a seven year programme, I realised I still had decades to go before I would see the fruition of my training. I didn't want to wait until my 60s to reap the rewards of my work! I thought about my dream of having a resort on a paradise island. I wanted that dream, but, even in 30 years, I wouldn't realise it as an architect. I knew I needed a different path to success. So I decided to quit college.

It was a hard decision, especially as my father had wanted me to be an architect. On the day I decided, I phoned him and said, "Dad, if I'm going to design buildings, it won't be as an architect. It will be as the person who owns the property and has the money to hire the best architects." I waited for his response.

He was surprised, and sounded disappointed, but, in the end, he said, "If that is what you have to do, go do it." I started my own company with a friend. We began a publishing business with almost no money and even less experience.

That's how I ended up in my late 20s, five years later, living in Singapore and running my little startup real estate property magazine. So much for making my life an instant success! I had dreams of wild wealth, but that dream's fulfilment seemed to lie in a hazy, distant future. I was falling ever deeper into debt. I was working very hard but paying myself very little. I felt like I had no choice. As the company grew, I had to hire another person, or pay for extra marketing to grow more. The way I saw it, once the business was successful, it would pay more. I believed I had to put money I made back into the business. The consequences of this decision were about to become clear in a very public way.

As I walked home one evening, lost in the thoughts of what I had to do, I noticed a commotion in our street. Someone was shouting. It sounded like crying. The neighbours were out watching the drama. As I walked closer, I saw they were looking at the front of our house. The one crying was Renata, my wife. Our daughter Kathleen, just a year old, and looking very distressed, was in Renata's arms. She was pleading with a man standing in front of a tow truck lifting our car up by its hook. I ran toward them. "You can't take our car. Please . . ." I heard Renata beg. She looked around and saw me.

"What's happening?' I asked, as if I didn't know. I had been late on the car payments again. Renata had reminded me, and I had promised to make a payment. But I hadn't. There simply wasn't enough money in the bank. Even though I was keeping up the appearance of being successful, in reality I was going into more debt each month, hoping it would all turn around one day. Now our money problems were out there for everyone to see. "We can pay you tomorrow!" I told the driver as they prepared to tow our car away.

He shook his head and handed us a pink slip. "Sign here" he said. "Call the number on the receipt."

I watched him drive off, and, humiliated, Renata walked back into the house. The neighbours cast me glances of pity, and then went back into their homes. I was alone now. No money, no car, and no self respect. Clearly I had been in denial about my business – ignorant of just how much stress it was causing my wife, my young family, and me. Standing on that empty street, I made a decision to change my priorities, once and for all. But how?

It wasn't that I hadn't tried before. I had read books that talked about paying yourself first, but none of them explained how I could make the money to pay myself in a way that was easy and natural. I had read books on success, leadership, and wealth creation, but the more I read, the more confused I became. Each new book's advice seemed to contradict the advice in the one I had just finished. One book stressed the importance of climbing the corporate ladder, while the next said you can't get wealthy from a job, and I'd be better off with my own business. Some said to follow my passion, while others told me to follow my purpose. Some urged me to be daring and take big, bold risks; others advised me to be cautious and to take small steps. Some said that the key to wealth was trading shares and options, while others dismissed that entirely, and recommended network marketing, online marketing or property investment.

Head spinning, I looked for suitable role models. That didn't work out any better. Richard Branson wrote that it is all about being the entrepreneur adventurer, but then Jack Welch proved you couldn't reach the top working for others. Oprah Winfrey showed the power of shining from the front with the stars, while Mark Zuckerberg was happy to hack in the back with his hoody. Warren Buffett and Bill Gates had entirely different paths to success. Buffett invests in many businesses, but never in anything high tech. Gates focused on growing just one high tech business.

Truth is, I had no idea what was right. Unable to find any clear direction, I ended up following the most common path: trial and error. That's how I ended up getting my car repossessed.

That night, in desperation, I made a decision. I was going to find my own path. That decision led me to find not only my path but also an entire map of wealth creation.

Fast forward a couple of decades, I am writing this book describing what I have learned since that night, from my dream resort in Bali. I have been living here for the better part of a decade, running a string of businesses and mentoring social entrepreneurs who are making an impact around the world.

I have made plenty of decisions, good and bad, to get here. But the quantum leap that put me on the path to wealth creation did not come when I had the dream, or when I had my first businesses. It was that evening in Singapore three years later when my car was repossessed, when I committed to the dream, and a clear plan to get there.

For the first time, I set a 'personal earning plan' that was more important to me than my business plan. Instead of paying myself less than I needed to survive, and hoping my businesses would one day make millions, I created a vision and a plan in which my personal net cash flow after expenses, increased every three months. Within a month, I was cash flow positive. Within six months, by keeping to my plan, I had an extra $500 every month, which I put aside. Over the next two years I kept to my plan, and my personal cash flow for investment grew to over $10,000 each month. Before I was 30 I had become a multi-millionaire, with the money and time to support the people and causes I believed in, simply as a result of changing my focus.

From my first business, as a teenager, to the dozen companies I built, sold, crashed, burned and grew in my 20s, to the thousands of people I mentored and worked with in my 30s, it became increasingly obvious to me that we all go through similar stages of learning, and similar breakthroughs, to master each stage of success. We are all on the same map, just in different places. This map – which I describe in detail in my book 'Millionaire Master Plan' (MMP) – is a three dimensional blueprint of a building the architect in me designed, which links to nine levels of wealth, from 'Victim' to 'Legend'. You and I are each at one of these levels. What we should do next depends on the level we are at.

Every one of us has a genius inside us. Once we realise it, we find our own internal guidance system. We are all on a journey together to improve our own wealth and the wealth of those around us. It's all about our ability to collectively create more and contribute more to the world. I call this mission 'World Wide Wealth'.

From 'The Millionaire Master Plan: Your Personalised Path to Finanical Success' by Roger James Hamilton. Copyright © 2014 by Roger James Hamilton. Used by permission of Business Plus, an imprint of Grand Central Publishing.

ABOUT THE AUTHOR
Teena Gates

Teena Gates is a published author, an experienced television and radio presenter, journalist and motivational speaker. Teena earned a reputation as an 'adventurist' after losing more than half her body weight in response to a health scare. From being clinically morbidly obese, Teena went on a journey, climbing to Everest Base Camp, and the summit of Island Peak in the Himalayas. She has climbed the French and Italian Alps, Mount Elgon (Uganda), Mount Elbrus (Russia), and Kilimanjaro, kayaked in The Nile, and trained as a long distance swimmer. She celebrated turning 50 by completing ten triathlons in one year.

"I've learned the value of pushing, of gasping for breath, of reaching for the light, the sun, and the world. There is a beautiful reward for crashing noisily into that prism of light."
TEENA GATES

How I Made A Rainbow

TEENA GATES

Fab, up to 50 – that's what life has been like. We all have ups and downs, but I'm lucky to have survived relatively intact. I've had a great job, I've had great love, I've travelled the world and had wonderful friends. I didn't have children, but that was intended. And I've written a book, earlier than expected, and about myself, which was never on my list of 'to-do's'. I've been 24 stone, and come down to eleven, losing more than half my bodyweight in a year. I've climbed huge mountains, and I've kayaked a white water rapid on the Nile.

Nevertheless, at the beginning of 2016, rather morbidly, I was looking at what I was bringing to my future. I'd collected a heap of weight, I was perimenopausal, had started my own business, and was busier than ever, far too busy, and I had terrific friends. I didn't feel 50, but I certainly felt fat.

Thinking of New Year resolutions, and wondering what to do to celebrate a changing decade, I got myself a 'Get up and Go' diary. It was filled with thoughtful snippets for every day. It was hard not to smile when opening a fresh day to a fresh thought and a new beginning. I'd been throwing around ideas of '50 things to do at 50' and I couldn't find anything that worked. It would have been easy to do loads of little things at 50, but that didn't quite fit the bill, and 50 'big' things didn't feel realistic in terms of time and money. Out of the blue, a challenge was thrown my way – to complete ten triathlons in a year. Ten triathlons to mark the start of a new decade had a ring to it!

With a lot of borrowed gear, and plenty of doubt, I dipped an actual toe into the pool in Carrick-On-Shannon for the Lough Key 'Try a Tri', my introduction to the world of triathlon. The encouragement of the people of Carrick cheering from the sidelines helped me to complete the course. That encouragement was something I became familiar with as I headed to Galway for the beautiful parkland and lake 'Lough Cutra Castle Triathlon'. In Athy, Co Kildare, I finished my first sprint distance triathlon during an Irish heatwave. As I ran along the river I thought I would die, but every elite athlete that passed shouted encouragement as I jogged along. I finished my fourth triathlon in Wexford and swam back across the bay afterwards just for the beauty of it. 'Hell's Angels' were born for number five, when I took my place in an all-girl team for a relay at Hell Of The West. My favourite run came in the lovely Dromineer with Nenagh Tri Club, followed by the Lakeside Tri in Donegal, King of Greystones in Wicklow, and triathlon number nine, the Salthill Tri in Galway.

People don't like me mentioning the 'F' word – but the truth is I was 'fat and 50' and feeling every ounce of it, as I squeezed myself into my lycra triathlon racing suit. But very quickly, I was reassured that I did have a place there. Throughout the year, I felt my confidence grow. Even though this is a hugely competitive sport, with amazing elites battling hard for position, I never felt left out. That was all down to Triathlon Ireland, its organising clubs, stewards, officials, safety crews, as well as the athletes and spectators who never stopped encouraging me along the way.

At the start, overweight and unable to run far, I felt quite a fraud turning up for my first 'try-a-tri' but nobody else saw me that way. Soon I realised that, even if I never won a race, I could win each time by performing better than the last. It wasn't only just about triathlon days. Everything counted, all the work and effort I put in between events, jogging on the road, swimming in the sea, cycling to work and going to the gym. And races weren't a judgement on how slow or bad I was, they were a celebration of how far I had come. Everybody encouraged me to realise that.

My tenth triathlon of the Summer, and my first full Olympic distance, started in Cobh. I was facing a 40km cycle and a 10km run, but more importantly, a full open sea swim from Spike Island back to Cobh. This stretch of water had fascinated me since, while working as a young radio reporter, the prison inmates had staged a riot, and I'd written about the prison population that then existed on the island. I'd thought of it as an Irish Alcatraz and often wondered what it would be like to swim for your freedom through those choppy, churning waters.

Those same waters were so rough on this final triathlon day that our swim was delayed as we waited for the safety officer to decide if it could go ahead. Eventually the 'green light' was given and, feeling slightly sick, I bounced along in a trawler as we were shipped out to Spike Island to start the swim to the mainland.

We climbed out of the boat and, heading down to the sandy beach, donned our coloured swim caps, and started a warm up. We listened carefully to the briefing about safety and tides, and how to call over a safety kayak if we found ourselves in difficulties, or wanted to end the swim. Adjusting our goggles, we headed for the sea and pushed off.

A curling wave crashed over me from behind, pushing me forward and below the surface. Through my goggles I caught a green, silent moment underwater, and had to remind myself to relax and pace my breathing. I kicked my legs, pushed my elbows back, and pulled my arm up through the wave as I restored my breath. Sunlight sparkled through droplets hurled from my hand, flashing a multi-coloured prism. Then it happened. I was swimming through rainbows

Glancing through the fierce swell, I spied the spire of Saint Colman's Cathedral to my right and, on my left, the smaller Christchurch Church of Ireland. I felt a spiritual connection to each, as if invisible tow-lines were guiding me back to shore. We were a perfect triangle, an unassailable power source, and the sea could not defeat me. In this moment, I was vibrantly alive, 50 years old, and definitely fabulous.

The wonderful support continued through the bike section, and finally the run, which actually ended as a walk and trot. But so many people shouted encouragement, and so many women came to walk and jog beside me, that I was almost overcome, as well as being happy and extremely grateful.

I'm so glad that I decided to 'Get up and Go' in my 50s. A whole marvellous decade lies ahead of me. At times it was touch and go as to whether I was ready to give in to feeling tired, heavy and deflated. I understand perfectly how easy that would be, like floating below the water line and letting go in the sea's calm, silent, green depths. But I've learned the value of pushing, of gasping for breath, of reaching for the light, the sun, and the world. There is a beautiful reward for crashing noisily into that prism of light. If you accept support, friendship, beauty, and, sometimes, the pain of life, and, if you gasp, and insist on coming up for air, you will find yourself living through rainbows.

ABOUT THE AUTHOR

Pádraic Ó Máille

Pádraic Ó Máille helps people and organisations to stand out, get noticed and achieve better results. He shows how you can realise infinitely more of your potential by improving your communication ability, and connecting better with your fellow human beings. He has worked with Entrepreneurs of the Year, Lions Rugby Captains and Government Taoisigh to express themselves more powerfully and realise more of their potential. His five keynote speeches and training programmes will seriously improve your sales, your service experience and your productivity. He is the bestselling author of two books: "The Midas Power", and "Rocking Horse Shit". His blog 'A Dose of Smácht' was singled out for the quality of its content by 256 Media in 2015. For more, see www.omaille.ie

"Between stimulus and response, there is a space. In that space is our power to choose our response. In our response lies our growth and our freedom."
VIKTOR FRANKL

Manage Your Wild Horses

PÁDRAIC Ó MÁILLE

"Pádraic. I need you to call me," the voice message said, a fairly innocuous communication if from your mother, or a client, or even your bank manager, but ominous in the extreme when from your cardiologist.

I replayed the message, hoping I had gotten it wrong. "Pádraic. I need you to call me."

The mind works powerfully to protect you from confrontation. It reminded me that I was driving to Thurles to present a talk to 60 business people in two hours time, that I needed to be utterly focused on that job, and should ring my cardiologist after lunch.

I listened again. There was no doubting the tone of voice, kind and caring, with a distinct, "Don't mess me about" edge. My mind whispered "D.I.N", an acronym for "Do It Now". Over the years I'd helped thousands of people to confront procrastination, getting them to affirm "Do It Now" whenever they put something off. It's probably the first thing I say to myself each morning when the alarm rings. I've programmed myself to counter seductive suggestions to press the snooze button by declaring "D.I.N." Once a champion snoozer, I rarely have a problem getting up first thing, whether or not I feel like it.

I muttered "D.I.N.," pulled off the road, dialled the number, and willed her to be anywhere but at that number.

"Pádraic, you didn't score an 'A' in your cardiac MRI". In a different context, I'd have loved that headline. David Ogilvy, the undisputed guru of the advertising industry, believed that a headline needed to fulfil four criteria – Grab Attention – Create Interest – Stimulate Desire – Get the client to take Action. My cardiologist had hit the bull's-eye on all four.

In the moments it had taken her to utter those words, my life stalled and dangled in suspense. I appeared to have unlimited time to assimilate the implications of those words.

I recalled earlier that month her prognosis on the angiogram she had performed on me. "Beautiful arteries Pádraic."

"What does that mean?" I asked innocently.

"It means, Pádraic, that your coronary arteries that supply blood to your heart are working perfectly, and you have no evidence of coronary artery disease." I got the message. It was neither her style nor preference to use more words than were necessary .

Now she was scoring me less than an 'A' in my cardiac MRI. It could be 84 or 4%. It provoked me to ask the first of what would be dozens of hard and uncomfortable questions. "What's the story? What's not perfect?"

"The MRI has detected that you may have left ventricular non-compaction."

It meant nothing. I scribbled it down on the unopened front page of the Irish Times on the passenger seat. I'd check it out later online and then deal with it.

"It also detected a nodule, or a mass, on your right atrium." That sounded exactly like cancer, and I hadn't a clue how to deal with that.

"I've contacted the 'go to' man in Ireland for this type of condition. He'll see you at 8pm on Friday in the Blackrock Clinic."

"Hang on a second." I said, with some assertiveness. "I've a gig on Friday."

If, in her best Mrs. Browne Dublin accent, she'd told me that "Denial isn't a river in Egypt", she'd have been forgiven. She paused for what seemed an eternity.

"I'll be there." I said.

In Gurtymadden, that bleak Tuesday morning, there were no restaurants open to purloin a sugary latte, no counselling clinics, and no bookshop with a book on what to do in times of trouble. The only things moving were about 12 untrained Connemara ponies frolicking in a paddock beside the roadside. A slip of a girl, in complete control of the madness and mayhem about her, was putting them through their paces.

The ponies were exuberant, skittish and unpredictable, prancing around the confining paddock. Some charged the robust fences in an effort to escape to different fields with sweeter, more tender grass. Others galloped around the same circle over and over again. I could see deep ruts and grooves appearing in the green meadow as they heedlessly acted on impulse. Others, listless and apathetic, lay on worn bedding, missing rugged, bleak Connemara where they'd spent the formative years of their life.

Their trainer, all of eight stone, was a consummate horse trainer. She had neither whip nor spur. Her only technology was a narrow gap in a wall that separated a bale of sweet hay from the ponies and her. Addressing each pony individually, she allowed some to enter the gap and indulge in the hay. Others were given further 'feedback' before being allowed access. Others again were not permitted to enter. To her, each wild pony was a champion in disguise waiting to be developed and unleashed. Over the coming minutes she transformed the behaviour and performance of many of those ponies.

I marvelled at how, with time and 'smácht' (the Irish word for discipline), she had each of those ponies jumping gracefully and happily through hoops and over fences. Many would be lauded for the unique and disciplined creatures they would become.

Like that paddock, my mind was one massive riot of panic. Right now, there was no trainer to calm, control, tame, harness or develop those wild horses.

All my life I'd been a worrier. As a kid I was terrorised by the boogie man lurking beneath my bed. As a teenager I despaired that girls would ever talk to me. As a student I stressed about failing every exam I ever took. As a business person I agonised over business drying up and going broke. I'd succeeded in overcoming many of those worries, and had achieved a modicum of success in certain circles.

From as far back as I can remember, I've been terrified of dying. My own father had died two months before I was born. A cousin of mine had been killed at 11, and, when I was 15, a close friend of mine died of a brain haemorrhage. I'd picture in vivid detail being assailed by every conceivable disease from A to Z, and each year would present to my GP with a new imagined ailment. Now I had an industrial strength health problem to worry about.

I recalled a line from the bible "And the thing I feared greatly has come upon me." I'd heard it said that about 60,000 thoughts or impulses cross our minds each day. Some are perfectly formed thoroughbreds, abundant with possibility, and capable of being trained to within an inch of their lives. Others lack the breeding, physique and temperament to ever achieve greatness. More again are destructive, dysfunctional and delusionary.

As I watched that girl patrol that little gap between the hay and the paddock, I was reminded of the iconic writer and psychiatrist Viktor Frankl. He had lost his wife and daughter to the Nazis under heinous circumstances, yet succeeded in retaining his sanity and purpose for life. In his book 'Man's Search for Meaning' he concludes that "Everything can be taken from a man but one thing, the last of the human freedoms, to choose one's attitude in any given set of circumstances, to choose one's own way" and "Between stimulus and response, there is a space. In that space is our power to choose our response. In our response lies our growth and our freedom."

The lesson of Gurtymadden was clear. We always have the power to choose our thoughts. The process of choosing your thoughts is simple. Stupid as it sounds, create a space to acknowledge and listen to each of your thoughts. The mere fact of slowing down thoughts creates a semblance of order and calm and control. Then decide which thoughts you allow to enter your reality. Similarly, decide which thoughts to ignore and dismiss.

The friskiest thought beating my door down right then was, "You've got cancer. Get back to Galway quick and down six pints to calm your nerves." I acknowledged that it was indeed possible I had cancer. One way or the other I would confirm that on Friday. In the meantime, I was going to usher it out of the 'paddock of my mind' and refuse to even consider it until Friday.

My next thought was equally demanding. "You're delivering a presentation on 'Positive Thinking' in Thurles in two hours where you're expected to light up the room. How are you going to pull yourself together for that when you'll probably be dead in three months?"

I had to give that thought serious credit. And I didn't have an answer. I sensed another pony, Joey the Clown, nuzzling at my fingers. I heard him whisper. "The show must go on. You'll be fine. Let go of the trapeze and trust."

And it does. And it will. And every step along the way, if you're open to them, Joey the Clowns will emerge from the universal ether to help you and guide you.

In times of trouble, your mind resembles a paddock of skittish, frantic, wild ponies. Remember that you can erect a little space where you vet, discipline and ultimately develop those thoughts. This simple process is the bedrock of modern psychotherapy.

My son Harry, an inveterate Liverpool fan, had given me a copy of Dr Steven Peters wonderful book 'The Chimp Paradox' early on in my troubles. Widely acclaimed as the guru behind Liverpool's excellent season in 2013/2014, Dr Peters concludes that your mind has at least two thinking machines – the frontal and the limbic – that independently interpret your experiences.

The frontal region is your conscious mind – your logical, rational and evidence-based centre. Your limbic is your wild pony or chimp, the emotional component of your brain that is paranoid, catastrophic and irrational. It dates from prehistoric times when its core function was to activate the 'Fight, flight or freeze' impulse. In that era those impulses were wholly appropriate, and oftentimes life-saving. Simultaneously, it can be your best friend and your worst enemy. While it can serve to protect you, frequently it will cause you to experience unnecessary panic and despair.

"Managing your impulsive, emotional chimp as an adult will be one of the biggest factors determining how successful you are in life," according to Dr Peters. Acknowledging your wild ponies or chimp is the first step. Communicating and listening to them is step two. Reassuring them with logical and rational facts is step three.

ABOUT THE AUTHOR
Jerry Cahill

The words advocate, hero and leader all describe Jerry Cahill. At 60 years old, Jerry believes that "exercise is the single most important thing in my life that keeps me healthy with CF." Cahill leads the Boomer Esiason Foundation's scholarship and grants division, and is the founder of Team Boomer – BEF's athletic and fund raising arm. His programme 'You Cannot Fail' includes a website and books. In 2016, to inspire others with CF, Jerry created 60:60, a goal to complete 60 activities on his "living list". People with CF share their stories on Club CF. The documentary 'Up for Air' followed his five-year journey through training, treatments, and a double lung transplant. For more, see www.cfwindsprints.com; www.jerrycahill.com; www.clubcysticfibrosis.com; www.youcannotfail.com; and www.teamboomer.org.

*"With my family behind me, I knew that
I could surmount anything that cystic fibrosis
threw in my path."*
JERRY CAHILL

You Cannot Fail:
A Story Of Cystic
Fibrosis

JERRY CAHILL

I was born into a large, loving family with a mom, dad, and siblings. We were a team, supportive of each other, and we were happy. Slowly however, my parents realised that I was different, that something was not quite right. So, they took me to a doctor, and I underwent a series of tests that eventually told us that I had Cystic Fibrosis, a chronic, genetic disease.

My parents' minds spun out with question after question. How could this happen? What are we going to do? How long will he live? Until, as always, they calmed down and formulated a plan based upon family, love and the belief that we could not fail. No matter what doctors told them about my health and apparent fragility, I was always encouraged to put family first and to spend as much time as possible with my siblings.

This love and family-first mentality that my parents instilled in me saved my life; it allowed me to live as normally as a child with cystic fibrosis could. I laughed, played, went to school, rough housed with my brothers, and I almost never felt different. My challenges were my own, as everyone's are, and, because of the foundation that my parents built, I thrived.

As I grew up, I developed a deep appreciation for athletics and exercise. Despite the fact that I was significantly smaller than my brothers, I played every sport that they did. From baseball to football, I trailed in their shadows striving to keep up and cultivating an all-important competitive drive until, eventually, I found that I could excel in pole vaulting. From this sport, I learned to be absolutely and completely relentless in every facet of my life. From school to athletics to my compliance with my health regime, I knew that to live, breathe, and succeed, I could never skip a step.

Throughout my teenage years, into college and adulthood, I implicitly believed that I could not fail and kept that idea to the forefront of my mind. With my family behind me, I knew that I could surmount anything that cystic fibrosis threw in my path. And so I did, from extra challenges during a long-lived pole vaulting career to facing down a forced, health-induced retirement from a job I not only loved, but had also put my entire being into, I remained resilient, and flourished by constantly moving forward and never looking in my rearview mirror.

Having devoted the greater part of my life to building a career in the fashion industry, and after climbing the corporate ladder to a Vice Presidential position, my body finally had enough. When that happened, it seemed to me that I had finally failed, that maybe, just maybe, I could not do everything I wanted to. The disease that I had for so long put to the side reared its ugly head and compelled me to take an action that I had no desire for – entering into early retirement and disability.

From that dark period came a new opportunity to keep moving onward in an even more impactful direction. I began to volunteer at the Boomer Esiason Foundation, a non-profit organisation dedicated to curing my disease – cystic fibrosis. And I then saw that my life could have a new direction, where I focused on my disease in the most positive way, and where, by sharing my own personal story, I could help others with CF overcome their own obstacles.

Ten years later, I am now the CF Ambassador for Educational Programs, Grants, and Team Boomer at the Boomer Esiason Foundation, a job I did not seek out. It fell into my path at a time when I felt hopeless. I have completely dedicated myself to building programmes that positively affect the CF community and contribute to people like me staying healthy, positive, and focused on moving forward.

At the Foundation, I discovered a new way that I could not fail, where I could demonstrate leadership and create new programmes that, had they been in existence during my journey, would have been useful to me. I founded the 'Team Boomer Program' that encourages people with cystic fibrosis to get out and exercise, something that I am truly passionate about because of the years I dedicated to pole vaulting and my own personal fitness and health. Every day, with the rest of the staff, I work to ensure that people with cystic fibrosis know that they can lead full lives, that they must exercise and stay medically compliant, and that, when life throws them a curve ball, they can forge a new path into the future.

While I was building this new path at the Boomer Esiason Foundation, I faced additional challenges with my own health. As typically happens with cystic fibrosis, my lung capacity deteriorated to a point that my lungs were no longer supporting my body. I needed a transplant. Not only had I lost my career, and a part of my identity, but my disease was also going to deprive me of a part of my physical body. But, as throughout my entire life, I fell back on what my parents taught me, to formulate a plan based on family, love and the thought that I could not fail. And I didn't.

Today, I am still here five years post-transplant, something only 50% of double lung transplant recipients can say. I continue to live every day at maximum capacity and to depend on family and the people who love me. No matter how sick I feel, or whatever new set of challenges my transplant throws up, I move forward continuously with unconquerable conviction.

My dedication to living in the here and now will always be with me, and my utter determination to live an unstoppable life at full throttle will never leave me. And I will always, always remember what my parents told me so many years ago… "Jerry, you cannot fail!"

ABOUT THE AUTHOR
Damien Brennan

Although brought up in Dublin, Damien Brennan is always a Sligo man. From a family that understands hospitality is not an industry but an illness, he has variously been a hotel manager, a publican, a fine-dining restaurateur and then for 20 years, a state tourism agency employee. From their private home overlooking the quintessential Yeatsian landscape of Lough Gill, he and his wife Paula Gilvarry host 'The Yeats Experience', bringing fine food, Yeats's Sligo heritage, and poetry to thousands of visitors every year. For more, see www.YeatsSligoIreland.com.

"From then on he knew that he'd make the very best he could of every talent and opportunity that life threw at him."

DAMIEN BRENNAN

The 12A

DAMIEN BRENNAN

As the eldest of four, he wasn't used to attention, nor did he expect it. Mother had much to do with the younger ones, and he was often expected to help. Today was going to be different. He was full of excitement. Three weeks out from his First Communion, he was being taken to the city centre to buy the suit. He was going to have her whole attention for a good part of the day, be made feel special and get his first matching outfit...

They took the 44 bus into Lower Harcourt Street and walked to Gorevan's Haberdashers and Outfitters of Camden Street. Not wanting to be considered a baby, he didn't hold her hand. The Gorevan brothers came from close to his mother's home place in Sligo, and she knew many of the sales people. If she was going to spend Dad's hard earned money then she considered it best to go to those she knew.

Michael Scanlon greeted them, glad to see her, and led them to the store's First Communion section. The wide selection was a challenge, but they soon settled on an appropriate suit, a three-piece in light grey tweed, its short trousers enhanced by a pair of knee-length grey socks held up with green ribboned elasticated trims. The boy was delighted. The new black shoes he'd got from the Kerry man in the shoe shop in Ranelagh weeks before would do fine.

The return journey allowed them to take the 12A from Camden Street to Kelly's Corner where they would meet up with the 44. The bus was packed. One raincoated, trilby-hatted man already clung to a leather strap by the two top seats. He noticed his mother noting him as they took their seats.

The next stop brought another man to an adjacent strap. The men knew each other.

"Well, Pat, it's an age since I bumped into you."

"Last time was at the Pro-Cathedral. Mahler, if I remember? Are you not coming back to us in the Culwick this year? We've begun rehearsing 'Dido and Aeneas'," the other responded.

"No, Our Lady's are doing a Bach Mass I've always wanted to sing, so I've jumped ship!"

"The new George Shiels is a great laugh at the Abbey. Have you seen it?"

"I have tickets for next Saturday and, by all reports, we're in for a treat. Well I'm off at the next stop, so till the next time." At that, the second man dropped the strap, making his way back down the swaying bus.

"Aren't some fellows great with all their interests," his mother said, her voice warm with feeling. At once he felt envious of her warmth, while almost understanding the admiration.

In the following moment came his first ever clear realisation. From then on he knew that he'd make the very best he could of every talent and opportunity that life threw at him.

Half an hour later they stepped off the 44 at their bus stop and turned into the suburban driveway towards home. Seeing strong smoke coming from their chimney, he was glad for his mother that the babysitter had kept the fire going. Within minutes they'd be back in the thick of the clamour of babies, and he'd revert to being responsible. His first big day out might be over, but he'd remember his lesson from the 12A for a lifetime.

ABOUT THE AUTHOR

Fiona Timoney

Raised on the other side of the world, Fiona had an extremely severe speech impediment, which was particularly unfortunate for her 'Aunty Tit.' At the age of 14, Fiona walked up the beach with a dead octopus stuck to her foot. At 18, she threw up on a dead cat, and at 24, she got knocked from her bicycle by a kangaroo. She once pulled a toaster from the table with her sandal at a fancy French restaurant. She regularly falls over and bumps into things, but only while sober. When she is not selling beautiful hand-crafted creations made from chocolate, she pictures all those who have aggrieved her over the years on her punching bag and drum-kit (just not at the same time). She lives in Sligo, Ireland, with Brendan, her extremely tolerant husband of 15 years. They have no kids or pets (but thanks for asking).

"My mission in life is not merely to survive, but to thrive; and to do so with some passion, some compassion, some humour, and some style."
MAYA ANGELOU

Cliff Jumping

FIONA TIMONEY

It would start in the shower, a slow buildup of tension in my chest until I almost couldn't breathe. I was totally taken aback. Despite many previous life stresses, I'd never suffered from anxiety before.

In July 2014 I was about to depart the city I had lived in for 43 years. I was going to leave the safety and security of friends and family, and streets I could navigate like the increasing lines on my face. With Brendan, my husband, I was about to abandon Canberra, Australia, for Sligo, Ireland, and a completely different life, to a house we had yet to see in person, bought on the basis of photos on the internet.

When we would tell people our plans, they would ask, "Why?" Why would we take such a massive step at our age and at this time in our lives? It was quite simple. The time had come to live a little and to take a risk.

For most of my life, I had taken the safe option. After studying law at the Australian National University, and getting a job as a criminal defence solicitor in private practice, I was involved in some high profile murder trials, and even found myself featured in a book, (since made into a film) about one of those trials. After ten years I left the stress and long hours behind to join the Australian Public Service. The hours were shorter, but the roles no less fascinating or stressful. My last position in Australia, before leaving for Ireland, involved working for a Royal Commission that requested a former Prime Minister to swear on the bible that he would tell the truth, the whole truth, and nothing but the truth, an almost impossible task for most politicians. While I had hoped that the change from private to public service would provide me with the job satisfaction I needed, something was sorely missing.

In 2013 Brendan and I came to visit his family in Co Fermanagh. We had been several times before, and had always loved our day trips to Sligo. This time we decided to spend a lot longer in Sligo town, and to immerse ourselves in the day to day lives of the people around us. One sunny summer's day, after a big night on the town, we went to the Peace Park next to the Cathedral, and lay in the sun eating raspberries and strawberries. With the sun on our faces, we fell asleep. When we awoke, an Arts Festival had set up right around us. There was a Punch and Judy Show, Tightrope Walkers, Belly Dancers and a Juggler, to name just a few. It felt like the whole thing had been set up for us. I recall saying that I had never felt happier in my whole life.

After four blissful weeks, we returned to Canberra, but nothing felt the same. I wasn't interested in accumulating more assets or possessions and found that most of the conversations around me no longer held my interest. Then, one evening, a documentary came on the television. It was about Benbulben, and, as the camera panned in front of that majestic mountain, I had a visceral reaction – I burst into tears. Right there and then I said to Brendan, 'That's where we have to move to.'

The only other spontaneous thing I have ever done was to marry Brendan after only six months together. When you know, you know, right? Thankfully, we have always seen eye to eye on the big stuff, like uprooting our entire lives and starting all over again. That night, we searched the internet until we found a house with a view of Benbulben, and our dream soon looked like becoming a reality.

The planets then aligned, and an opportunity to do something totally different in our work lives presented itself. We are now the Directors of Lollypotz Ireland, which takes chocolates and custom-makes them into beautiful floral bouquets. This is a million miles away from what I used to do for a living. Although running your own business has many and varied challenges, I love being my own boss. Most importantly, we now get to live in a part of the world whose natural beauty needs to be seen to be believed.

Back in 2014, it all felt like jumping off a very high sea cliff. The prospect of that leap took my breath away, but I was confident that deep enough water would break my fall, and I would be able to dogpaddle my way to safety. Now, in 2017, I see that I've done considerably better than dog-paddle. If I were to take the time to float on my back looking up at the sky, one thought would dominate – life's too short to spend any part of it doing what makes you unhappy. Take that leap. It could be the best thing you've ever done.

ABOUT THE AUTHOR

Eileen Forrestal

For most of her life Eileen stuttered badly and chose a profession and specialty (anaesthesia) that allowed her to hide from social interactions. After meeting its publisher in 2006, Eileen transformed 'The Irish Survivors Diary' business into 'The Irish Get Up and Go Diary'. The Get Up and Go diaries provide a source of timeless wisdom from a "pre-information age" to guide people through the challenges of modern life and "shine a light in the darkness of despair". Eileen overcame her fear of public speaking to get her message of 'Get up and go' into the world. An appearance on RTÉ's Dragons' Den in 2011 was a baptism of fire, and she has not looked back since. Having graduated from UCD in 1982, Eileen practiced medicine in the UK, Zambia and Canada before returning to Ireland in 1995. A passionate traveller and mini-adventurer, she has visited over 50 countries including a trip 'around the world in 85 days'. She lives in Sligo with her partner Brendan (whom she met on a fundraising trip to Everest Base camp in 2002) and her crazy cocker spaniel, Kellie.

*"The cave you fear to enter holds
the treasure you seek."*
JOSEPH CAMPBELL

Yes, You Can!

EILEEN FORRESTAL

During a weekend seminar I attended – somebody suggested that, with my marriage recently over, it might be interesting, or even beneficial – I suddenly realised that what came out of my mouth could design my life; that what I said could make a real difference. That was a scary thought.

It seems obvious now, but then, when I spoke, I was mostly explaining, arguing, complaining or describing something that happened, or mindlessly repeating what I had previously said or heard. I pondered it a while, went back to work and tried to forget about it.

Deep down, I didn't believe that I had anything important to say. Because of a childhood stammer, speaking was difficult. My life became about what words I could and could not say, about trying to fit in and be normal, and trying to be understood. I had spent my life watching and listening to others doing, so easily, something that, for me, seemed impossible. If what I had to say could actually make a difference, I didn't even want to think about that.

Soon after, in my local supermarket, I spotted a gentlemen I recognised as someone who was featured regularly in the local paper for taking groups to Kenya to climb Kilimanjaro to fundraise for Childaid in support of a school in the Mukuru slums of Nairobi. Although we worked in the same hospital, we had never met. As he was not a young man, I had always admired his commitment. On impulse, I decided to approach him and acknowledge him for the great work he was doing.

I had barely introduced myself when he asked, "So, would you like to come on our next trip? We are going in March."

I was stopped in my tracks. My usual response, to react with a nice platitude and decline, didn't come.

"You would need to raise €3,000 for Childaid," he continued.

I visualised two 'cartoon bubbles' coming from my mouth – and a choice – acutely aware that what came from this minute mattered and could determine my future.

I had any amount of excuses and reasons not to – fundraising was not my thing; I wasn't a climber; I had no holidays; I couldn't take a month off at short notice; and I didn't want to climb Kilimanjaro!

"Okay. Yes. Sure." I wasn't a bit sure!

"That's great," he said. "I'll be in touch."

Now came the practicalities. I had to negotiate the work roster to get the necessary time off. A visit to the general manager, a request for unpaid leave, and a promise to do extra sessions, sorted that.

The fundraising target of €3,000 was more difficult. I hated asking for money, especially if there was a possibility that I might enjoy the climb. However, every cent that I raised would not be raised, were I not willing to take on this challenge. That money would make a world of difference to those students in Mukuru slum school. It was worth a few raised eyebrows!

I used the daily inspirations in my 'Irish Survivor's Diary' – now 'The Irish Get Up and Go Diary' – to keep me on track with training and fundraising, especially on dark days, when it no longer seemed like a good idea.

I climbed Knocknarea a few times, and spent many non-fun evenings walking uphill on the treadmill in the local gym. I would climb as high as possible, I decided, and then turn around and come home.

One fundraising effort included a 'sponsored silence' by a class in a school where my cousin taught. In return for me returning to the school to tell them all about my experience, they would raise money. A legacy of my childhood stammer was that public speaking, in any shape or form, held a certain terror. Up until this point, I had managed to avoid it. But I needed the funds, and it wasn't about me. So, with dread in the pit of my stomach, another 'cartoon bubbles' vision, a different 'yes or no' choice, and a memory from the weekend seminar – 'Feel the fear and do it anyway' – I said yes, and, for the first time, knew that I would honour my word, and not allow fear to stop me.

Five months after that fateful encounter with Pat at the dairy counter, I was funded, reasonably fit, ready, and probably able, to take on Kilimanjaro. And I could opt out, as I had no intention of dying on any mountain!

The first three days, with keen, fun groups of people from all over Ireland, were fabulous. We had sunshine, camaraderie, good conversations, and lots of stories, jokes and suggestions. The pace was perfect – all poli, poli (slowly, slowly) – with the instruction that, if you thought you were going slowly, to go even slower! As we rose through the changing terrain, the climb was not tough.

Higher up the air became thinner. More effort was required. The chat became less exuberant, but spirits remained high, despite aching limbs, damp clothing, and increasing tiredness from poor sleep in makeshift huts.

On the fourth day, as we approached Kibo hut, I was exhausted. It was extremely cold, and snow looked imminent. The plan was to have a snack, then sleep until midnight, when we would begin the ascent to the top in time for sunrise.

I couldn't eat much as the altitude was causing unpleasant nausea, and my headache was becoming severe. I knew the dangers of cerebral and pulmonary oedema. Not wanting to take chances, I took the Diamox I had brought, along with two paracetamol, and went straight to bed. As I made my way to my bunk at the back of the room, my clumping boots disturbed people trying to sleep. I hoisted myself onto the top bunk, peeled off layers of heavy outdoor clothing, pulled on leggings, thermals, socks, gloves, hoodie, wriggled into my sleeping bag, closed it tightly over my head and tried to warm up. Suddenly I needed to go to the toilet.

Fighting tears of annoyance, I got out of the sleeping bag, divested myself of my night attire, replaced it with outdoor garments, negotiated the steps, and again clumped across the room to angry mutterings from the bunks of those struggling to sleep. Outside, in freezing darkness, it was snowing heavily. I made my way to the edge of the world. Unable to face the nauseating stench of the latrine, I located somewhere fresher. My freezing fingers struggled with my trousers zip, until I eventually succeeded in relieving my massively stretched bladder.

I returned to the building, walked back across the wooden floor, got up into the bunk, put on my night attire and slipped into the sleeping bag. Thirty seconds later I knew I needed to go again.

Five times in total I made that journey during the six hours I was supposed to be sleeping. I realised that Diamox was a diuretic that was actively flushing any excess fluid due to the altitude from my system.

By the time the ascent at midnight was to start, I was wrecked. There was no way I would be reaching the top of any Kilimanjaro. I had to tell somebody I had had no sleep, was exhausted and frozen, probably suffering from altitude sickness (although my headache was gone), and needed to descend quickly.

I heard disembodied voices in the pitch dark. I looked all around and couldn't see anyone, nor any of their head lights, but I could hear them. I looked up. There, like a string of lights on a high wall, the rest of the group was winding its way up the mountain.

Then suddenly, beside me, a massive smile and two bright eyes shone out of the darkness.

"Hello, I'm Douglas. I will be your guide."

"That's great Douglas, but I need to go down."

"It's okay. You can do it. We go this way." And he headed off up over rocks.

I climbed two steps up what seemed like a steep stairs. I stopped. "I can't do it, Douglas. I just can't."

"It's okay. You can do it. I will help you. Just one more step."

I took another step. "I can't. It's too steep. It's too cold." and took another. Slowly and painfully, I put one foot in front of the other, climbing. Each time I stopped, begging and pleading, "I will die on this mountain," he smiled.

"You are okay, you can do it, just one more step."

I hadn't the energy to argue. I surrendered. He walked with me for ten hours.

Every time I faltered, he simply said, "It's okay, you can do it. Don't sleep. One more step."

I stumbled, cried, wanted to sit down and sleep but, step by step, we inched forward. As the darkness eased, I could make out the early morning pre-dawn landscape below and, as the sun came up, the Serengeti woke to a new day. It was astonishingly beautiful. I was overwhelmed. As we ascended into the clouds, then rose above them, it was truly a magical moment.

And then I saw someone below me. One of our group, also with his guide, was painstakingly navigating the steep, rocky terrain. With renewed courage, and numbed beyond any experience of cold, I continued.

We met the rest of our group already on the descent. "Go on, you're brilliant, you're nearly there, you can do it. It's worth it, keep going," they shouted.

Three hours later I arrived at the top of Kilimanjaro. We waited 30 minutes for the other climbers. Beside ourselves with pride, we took a photo, then set off on a rapid descent, arm in arm, running, laughing, and bringing snow, stones and rocks with us. I did it. Douglas did it. We did it. And it was Douglas's encouragement that had me do it. He knew I could. I didn't. I believed that I couldn't. I was ready to sell out on myself. Only I couldn't fight him, so I had to trust him. Sometimes others are a greater stand for us than we are for ourselves.

We visited the slum school, met the excited students, and handed over the money we had raised. Without a shadow of a doubt, their lives would not be the same, nor mine.

"You have succeeded in reaching the top of Kilimanjaro. We are going to trek to Everest's Base Camp in November. Will you come?" came at the end.

"Yes. Sure." And I did.

Back in Ireland, I visited my cousin's school, and told the students everything about the trip.